PUFFIN BOOKS
THE BOURNVITA QUIZ CONTEST
COLLECTOR'S EDITION: VOLUME 2

Derek O'Brien is an author, television personality, public speaker, politician and quizmaster.

Born in Kolkata, he began his career as a journalist for *Sportsworld* magazine but soon shifted to advertising. After working for a number of very successful years as the creative head of Ogilvy, Derek decided to focus all his energy and talent on his passion—quizzing.

Today, Derek is Asia's best-known quizmaster and the CEO of Derek O'Brien & Associates. He has been the host of the longest-running game show on Indian television, the *Bournvita Quiz Contest*, for which he was voted Best Anchor of a Game Show at the Indian Television Academy Awards three years in a row. Always innovating, Derek is also credited with having conducted the first quiz on Twitter in 2010.

Derek is a twice-serving member of the Rajya Sabha from West Bengal. He is the parliamentary party leader of the All India Trinamool Congress in the Rajya Sabha as well as the chief national spokesperson of the party. He has spoken at, among others, Harvard, Yale and Columbia universities in the United States as well as several IIMs, IITs and other premier educational institutions in India. He addressed the United Nations General Assembly as a member of the Indian parliamentary delegation in 2012. He has written over sixty bestselling reference, quiz and school textbooks.

To know more about the author, visit his website www.derek.in. You can also follow him on Twitter, Instagram and Facebook (@derekobrienmp).

READ MORE IN PUFFIN BY THE SAME AUTHOR

Discover with Derek (Primer, Parts I–III)
Cadbury Bournvita Book of Knowledge (Books 1–14)
The Best of Cadbury Bournvita Quiz Contest
The Puffin Factfinder
The Bournvita Quiz Contest Collector's Edition: Volume 1

THE

COLLECTOR'S EDITION
VOLUME 2

DEREK O'BRIEN

PUFFIN BOOKS

An imprint of Penguin Random House

PUFFIN BOOKS

USA | Canada | UK | Ireland | Australia
New Zealand | India | South Africa | China

Puffin Books is part of the Penguin Random House group of companies
whose addresses can be found at global.penguinrandomhouse.com

Published by Penguin Random House India Pvt. Ltd
7th Floor, Infinity Tower C, DLF Cyber City,
Gurgaon 122 002, Haryana, India

First published in Puffin Books by Penguin Random House India 2021

Copyright © Derek O'Brien & Associates 2021

10 9 8 7 6 5 4 3 2 1

ISBN 9780143447016

Typeset in Bauer Grotesk Pro by Manipal Technologies Limited, Manipal
Book design by Parag Chitale
Printed at Replika Press Pvt. Ltd, India

www.penguin.co.in

CONTENTS

ART AND CULTURE

1. The name of the folk dance garba comes from a Sanskrit word meaning ...
   a) Incense stick
   b) Lamp inside a pot
   c) Spiral movement
   d) Garland

2. The archaeological evidence of which dance form, dating back to the second century BCE, is found in the caves of Udayagiri and Khandagiri near Bhubaneswar?
   a) Manipuri
   b) Kathak
   c) Odissi
   d) Kathakali

3. 'www.sarod.com' is the official website of which musician?
   a) Amjad Ali Khan

b) Zakir Hussain
c) Hariprasad Chaurasia
d) Ravi Shankar

4. Which of these theatre forms originated in Kerala?
   a) Nautanki
   b) Koodiyattam
   c) Bhavai
   d) Bhaona

5. In which state is the Mamallapuram Dance Festival celebrated?
   a) Kerala
   b) Andhra Pradesh
   c) Tamil Nadu
   d) Uttar Pradesh

6. In Kathakali, who among these wears a special crown decorated with peacock feathers?
   a) Kamsa
   b) Ravana
   c) Shishupala
   d) Krishna

7. Which animal has become a central part of M.F. Husain's paintings since the 1950s?
   a) Horse
   b) Lion
   c) Dragon
   d) Rat

8. In which dance form is the dancer usually dressed in a white and gold-bordered kasavu sari?
   a) Odissi
   b) Kathak
   c) Mohiniattam
   d) Manipuri

9. What is known as *kolam* in Tamil Nadu, *mandana* in Rajasthan and *aripana* in Bihar?
   a) Sari
   b) Carpet
   c) Rangoli
   d) Roti

10. Which of these is a stringed instrument?
   a) Ektara
   b) Tabla
   c) Mridangam
   d) Bansuri

11. Putul Nautch is the traditional rod puppet art form of which state of India?
   a) Kerala
   b) Haryana
   c) Punjab
   d) West Bengal

12. Warli paintings are generally painted on a mud base using one colour, which is . . .
   a) White
   b) Blue

c) Green

d) Orange

13. In which of these art forms are characters grouped as *pacha*, *kathi* and *thadi*?

a) Kathak

b) Bharatanatyam

c) Kuchipudi

d) Kathakali

14. Traditionally, the white colour used in Madhubani paintings is obtained from ...

a) Milk

b) Curd

c) Rice

d) Paneer

15. The Natyanjali Nritya Utsav celebrated in Chidambaram, Tamil Nadu is dedicated to ...

a) Nataraja

b) Vishnu

c) Brahma

d) Menaka

16. Of all of the portraits painted by Leonardo da Vinci in Florence, how many survive till date?

a) One

b) Five

c) Twenty

d) None

17. In 2010, M.F. Husain was conferred the nationality of . . .
   a) Qatar
   b) Oman
   c) Germany
   d) South Africa

18. In which state is the Khajuraho Dance Festival held?
   a) Uttar Pradesh
   b) Madhya Pradesh
   c) Rajasthan
   d) Kerala

19. Which of these artists first sang at the age of twelve for the Assamese film *Indramalati*?
   a) Shah Rukh Khan
   b) Jagjit Singh
   c) Kishore Kumar
   d) Bhupen Hazarika

20. Which of these dance forms originated in Tamil Nadu?
   a) Kathak
   b) Bharatanatyam
   c) Kuchipudi
   d) Odissi

ASTRONOMY

1. Which of these planets is not named after Greek or Roman gods and goddesses?
    a) Mars
    b) Uranus
    c) Venus
    d) Earth

2. With which planet of the solar system would you associate the Cassini Division?
    a) Uranus
    b) Saturn
    c) Neptune
    d) Jupiter

3. If you were on Venus, from which direction would you see the sun rising?
    a) North

b) South
c) West
d) East

4. Since its discovery, which planet completed its first revolution around the sun in 2011?
   a) Mars
   b) Titan
   c) Earth
   d) Neptune

5. Who is credited as being the first person to look at the moon through a telescope?
   a) Christopher Columbus
   b) Galileo Galilei
   c) Alexander Graham Bell
   d) Stephen Hawking

6. Which was the most distant planet from the sun before the discovery of Pluto in 1930?
   a) Jupiter
   b) Saturn
   c) Mercury
   d) Neptune

7. The heaviest of all, this planet also rotates faster than all the others. Name it.
   a) Jupiter
   b) Venus
   c) Mercury
   d) Neptune

8. Which planet was known in ancient Greece by two different names—Phosphorus, when it appeared as a morning star, and Hesperus, when it appeared as an evening star?
a) Venus
b) Mercury
c) Jupiter
d) Mars

9. Apart from Uranus, which planet was discovered after the invention of the telescope?
a) Neptune
b) Venus
c) Jupiter
d) Earth

10. The atmosphere of Saturn is made up mostly of hydrogen and ...
a) Methane
b) Ammonia
c) Chlorine
d) Helium

11. On which planet would you come across the Great Red Spot?
a) Jupiter
b) Saturn
c) Neptune
d) Mars

12. In which World Heritage Site would you find instruments called *digamsa* and *nadivalaya*?
a) Jantar Mantar

b) Gol Gumbaz
c) Golconda Fort
d) Charminar

13. The windiest planet in the solar system, which takes 165 Earth-years to revolve around the sun is ...
a) Uranus
b) Saturn
c) Neptune
d) Jupiter

14. Who published his telescopic observations in a paper called *The Starry Messenger*?
a) Johannes Kepler
b) Galileo Galilei
c) Socrates
d) Julius Caesar

15. Who wrote *Six Books Concerning the Revolutions of the Heavenly Orbs*?
a) Galileo Galilei
b) Nicolaus Copernicus
c) Tycho Brahe
d) Isaac Newton

16. In western astronomy, which zodiacal constellation lies between Aries and Gemini?
a) Taurus
b) Libra
c) Leo
d) Scorpio

17. The constellation Ursa Major is also known as . . .
   a)   The Great Bear
   b)   The Little Dog
   c)   The Lion
   d)   The Big Cat

18. What are sometimes called minor planets?
   a)   Moons
   b)   Comets
   c)   Meteors
   d)   Asteroids

19. Ariel, Miranda and Oberon are the moons of which planet?
   a)   Neptune
   b)   Mars
   c)   Uranus
   d)   Jupiter

20. Who is credited with discovering Ganymede, the largest moon in our solar system?
   a)   Christiaan Huygens
   b)   Edmond Halley
   c)   Galileo Galilei
   d)   Leonardo da Vinci

AWARDS

1. In Madhya Pradesh, a person is awarded the Tansen Samman for contributing to the field of . . .
   a) Classical music
   b) Literature
   c) Sports
   d) Physics

2. Whose film, *Through the Eyes of a Painter*, won the Golden Bear award at the 1967 Berlin International Film Festival?
   a) Satyajit Ray
   b) M.F. Husain
   c) R.K. Laxman
   d) Jamini Roy

3. Till 2019, who was the last non-Indian to have been awarded the Bharat Ratna?
   a) Winston Churchill

b) George Washington
c) Khan Abdul Ghaffar Khan
d) Nelson Mandela

4. For which film did Karan Johar win the Filmfare Best Director Award in 2011?
a) *Kuch Kuch Hota Hai*
b) *My Name Is Khan*
c) *Kal Ho Naa Ho*
d) *Taare Zameen Par*

5. Which is the highest literary award in India?
a) Vyas Samman
b) Sahitya Akademi Award
c) Jnanpith Award
d) Premchand Fellowship

6. Who was the first sitting member of the Rajya Sabha to receive the Bharat Ratna?
a) Atal Bihari Vajpayee
b) Sachin Tendulkar
c) Lata Mangeshkar
d) Indira Gandhi

7. Which Indian was awarded the Ramon Magsaysay Award in 1958 and the Bharat Ratna in 1983?
a) Vinoba Bhave
b) M.S. Subbulakshmi
c) Mother Teresa
d) Baba Amte

8. In India, the Sant Kabir Award is conferred upon members of which profession?
   a) Fishermen
   b) Poets
   c) Singers
   d) Weavers

9. Who among the following prime ministers has not received the Bharat Ratna?
   a) Lal Bahadur Shastri
   b) Rajiv Gandhi
   c) Indira Gandhi
   d) V.P. Singh

10. Who was the first person to receive the Sahitya Akademi Award for writing in English?
   a) Amitav Ghosh
   b) R.K. Narayan
   c) Vikram Seth
   d) Arundhati Roy

11. Who was the first sportsperson to receive the Rajiv Gandhi Khel Ratna?
   a) Sunil Gavaskar
   b) Viswanathan Anand
   c) P.T. Usha
   d) Sania Mirza

12. Which Bharat Ratna awardee played the shehnai in the 1959 film *Goonj Uthi Shehnai*?
   a) Zakir Hussain

b) Bismillah Khan
c) Ravi Shankar
d) Hariprasad Chaurasia

13. Who was the first Indian to win two Academy Awards?
a) Bhanu Athaiya
b) Satyajit Ray
c) A.R. Rahman
d) Mrinal Sen

14. Till 2016, apart from C.V. Raman and A.P.J. Abdul Kalam, who was the only person to be awarded the Bharat Ratna for his contribution to science?
a) Homi Bhabha
b) C.N.R. Rao
c) Jagadish Chandra Bose
d) Vikram Sarabhai

15. Who was the first actress to win the National Film Award for Best Actress?
a) Nargis Dutt
b) Madhubala
c) Hema Malini
d) Waheeda Rehman

16. The medal of which award shows four replicas of 'Indra's Vajra' with the state emblem embossed in the centre?
a) Ashok Chakra
b) Kirti Chakra
c) Shaurya Chakra
d) Param Vir Chakra

17. In 1919, who renounced his knighthood following the Jallianwala Bagh massacre?
a) Jawaharlal Nehru
b) Mahatma Gandhi
c) Rabindranath Tagore
d) B.R. Ambedkar

18. Who received the Filmfare Lifetime Achievement Award in 1991?
a) Dilip Kumar
b) Amitabh Bachchan
c) Rajesh Khanna
d) Lata Mangeshkar

19. Which award was bestowed upon Mother Teresa in 1962, Verghese Kurien in 1963 and Arvind Kejriwal in 2006?
a) Ramon Magsaysay Award
b) International Gandhi Peace Prize
c) Deming Prize
d) Peabody Awards

20. Which prize was created in 1951 following a donation from Biju Patnaik?
a) Nandi Awards
b) Kalinga Prize
c) Kalidas Samman
d) Kumar Gandharva Award

BOOKS AND AUTHORS

1. Who published his first poems at the age of sixteen under the pseudonym Bhanushingho, meaning 'the Sun Lion'?
    a) Pranab Mukherjee
    b) Rabindranath Tagore
    c) Bankim Chandra Chatterjee
    d) Kazi Nazrul Islam

2. The television series *Bharat Ek Khoj* was based on a book written by . . .
    a) Jawaharlal Nehru
    b) C. Rajagopalachari
    c) Rajendra Prasad
    d) Subhas Chandra Bose

3. *The Tunnel of Time* is the autobiography of which author and cartoonist?
    a) R.K. Laxman

b) Amrita Pritam
c) Mulk Raj Anand
d) Mario Miranda

4. Which is the fourth and last Veda?
a) Rig Veda
b) Sama Veda
c) Atharva Veda
d) Yajur Veda

5. The book *Singhasan Battisi* relates the story of which king?
a) Vikramaditya
b) Shivaji
c) Maharana Pratap
d) Akbar

6. The 547 stories of the Jataka Tales are a part of the scriptures of which religion?
a) Jainism
b) Buddhism
c) Judaism
d) Islam

7. *Swami and Friends* was the first novel to be set in which imaginary town?
a) Timbuktu
b) Malgudi
c) Agrabah
d) Dholakpur

8. Which of these films is loosely based on Chetan Bhagat's book *Five Point Someone*?
a) *Munnabhai M.B.B.S.*
b) *3 Idiots*
c) *Patiala House*
d) *Lagaan*

9. Who among these was famous for writing *dohas*?
a) Kabir
b) Aryabhata
c) Ashoka
d) Tenali Rama

10. Which film director designed the covers of the Bengali translation of Jim Corbett's *Man-Eaters of Kumaon*?
a) Rabindranath Tagore
b) Ravi Shankar
c) R.K. Laxman
d) Satyajit Ray

11. Which of these characters was not created by Agatha Christie?
a) Thomas Beresford
b) Perry Mason
c) Parker Pyne
d) Hercule Poirot

12. In which of these books would you meet the Frog-Footman and the Mock Turtle?
a) *David Copperfield*
b) *Alice's Adventures in Wonderland*

c) *Black Beauty*
d) *Animal Farm*

13. In *The Jungle Book*, who was regarded as the weakest living thing on Earth by Father Wolf?
a) Tiger
b) Wolf
c) Man
d) Snake

14. 'Whether I shall turn out to be the hero of my own life, or whether that station will be held by anybody else, these pages must show.' These are the opening lines of which famous book?
a) *David Copperfield*
b) *The Count of Monte Cristo*
c) *The Adventures of Huckleberry Finn*
d) *Gulliver's Travels*

15. Más a Tierra, the island on which the Royal Navy officer Alexander Selkirk was trapped for many years, has been renamed...
a) Robinson Crusoe Island
b) Treasure Island
c) Captain Nemo Island
d) Gulliver Island

16. Which of these books was originally titled *Travels into Several Remote Nations of the World*?
a) *Gulliver's Travels*
b) *Around the World in Eighty Days*

c) *The Three Musketeers*
d) *Black Beauty*

17. On his last voyage, which literary character was asked to collect tusks of 500 elephants?
a) Gulliver
b) Sinbad
c) Aladdin
d) Phileas Fogg

18. In *Ali Baba and the Forty Thieves*, what was Ali Baba's profession?
a) Milkman
b) Woodcutter
c) Goldsmith
d) Cobbler

19. In which book would you meet a young boy named Jim Hawkins who helps his parents run the Admiral Benbow, an inn near Bristol?
a) *Robinson Crusoe*
b) *Ivanhoe*
c) *Gulliver's Travels*
d) *Treasure Island*

20. Which of these novels is set in the Third Age of Middle Earth?
a) *The Lord of the Rings*
b) *Harry Potter and the Philosopher's Stone*
c) *The Chronicles of Narnia*
d) *Breaking Dawn*

CLOTHES AND ACCESSORIES

1. The bells on ghungroos are usually made of which metal?
    a) Silver
    b) Brass
    c) Copper
    d) Iron

2. The name of which precious stone owes its origin to the Latin word for 'seawater'?
    a) Turquoise
    b) Aquamarine
    c) Emerald
    d) Topaz

3. Around AD 550, Justinian I persuaded two Persian monks from China to smuggle what to Constantinople in the hollows of their bamboo canes?
    a) Tea leaves

b) Papyrus
c) Leather shoes
d) Silkworms

4. The name of which gemstone comes from a Greek word meaning 'invincible'?
a) Pearl
b) Ruby
c) Diamond
d) Sapphire

5. Loafer, pump and wedge are all types of . . .
a) Hats
b) Jackets
c) Shoes
d) Umbrellas

6. What are pencil, toothbrush and handlebar types of?
a) Skirts
b) Moustaches
c) Heels
d) Hairstyles

7. Who won the first Filmfare Award for Costume Design in 1995?
a) Rohit Khosla
b) Ritu Kumar
c) Satya Paul
d) Manish Malhotra

8. Which animal's hair is used to make the mohair yarn?
   a) Goat
   b) Rabbit
   c) Elephant
   d) Yak

9. Which of these is a part of the traditional dress for men in Scotland?
   a) Kebaya
   b) Kilt
   c) Kimono
   d) Kaftan

10. In Assam, on which part of the body would you wear a *jaapi* made from bamboo?
   a) Head
   b) Nose
   c) Ankle
   d) Waist

11. Which of these is a knee-length coat that buttons to the neck and is worn by men from South Asia?
   a) Sherwani
   b) Mekhala
   c) Poncho
   d) Capri

12. On which part of the body is a jhanjhar worn?
   a) Neck
   b) Ears

c) Wrist
d) Ankle

13. If jodhpurs are trousers for horse riding, then what are patialas?
a) Teacups
b) Pleated salwars
c) Embroidered bags
d) Painted carpets

14. Which of these is an eye cosmetic?
a) Surma
b) Gajra
c) Bindi
d) Kundal

15. On which part of the body would you generally wear a beanie?
a) Wrist
b) Head
c) Ankle
d) Waist

16. Which of the following is a textile dyeing technique native to the island of Java?
a) Chikankari
b) Batik
c) Phulkari
d) Ikat

17. Phulkari, meaning 'flower work', is a type of …
a) Embroidery
b) Sculpture

c) Paper-folding technique
d) Flower arrangement

18. What are spread, button-down, forward point and club types of?
a) Collars
b) Skirts
c) Shoes
d) Sleeves

19. The word 'pashmina' comes from the Persian word for . . .
a) Silk
b) Cotton
c) Wool
d) Jute

20. Which of these items of clothing is not named after an island?
a) Capris
b) Bermudas
c) Cargos
d) Hawaiian shirts

CARTOONS AND COMICS

1. Name the stuffed pet tiger of the cartoon character Calvin.
   a) Hobbes
   b) Ruff
   c) Hot Dog
   d) Snoopy

2. Who is the CEO of Wayne Enterprises?
   a) Spider-Man
   b) Batman
   c) Captain America
   d) Superman

3. In which of these shows would you meet a character named Ash Ketchum?
   a) Pokémon
   b) Ninja Hattori

c) Doraemon
d) Archie Comics

4. Which superhero was born in Forest Hills, New York?
a) Phantom
b) Spider-Man
c) Superman
d) Captain Vyom

5. In Chacha Chaudhary comics, it is said that every time Sabu loses his temper, a volcano erupts on ...
a) Jupiter
b) Saturn
c) Earth
d) Venus

6. Which superhero was born when Victor Stone met with an accident and his scientist father saved him by replacing more than half his body with cybernetic parts?
a) Cyborg
b) Iron Man
c) Hulk
d) Wolverine

7. Which superhero got his superpowers when he was caught in a gamma bomb explosion while trying to save a teenager's life?
a) Thor
b) Hulk
c) Iron Man
d) Captain America

8. In comics, whose body is enhanced by the modified techno-organic virus, Extremis?
a) Superman
b) Spider-Man
c) Batman
d) Iron Man

9. Which comic-strip character has a brain that works faster than a computer?
a) Chacha Chaudhary
b) Suppandi
c) Pavitr Prabhakar
d) Shaktimaan

10. If Hero is Phantom's pet horse, what kind of animal is Devil?
a) Lion
b) Wolf
c) Camel
d) Cheetah

11. What is the name of the talking monkey in the Chhota Bheem series?
a) Kalia
b) Raju
c) Chutki
d) Jaggu

12. Which superhero's sketches made by artist Bob Kane showed him with wings and red tights?
a) Spider-Man
b) Superman

c) Batman
d) Shaktimaan

13. What breed is Tintin's dog?
a) Boxer
b) Fox terrier
c) Greyhound
d) Chihuahua

14. In the Tom and Jerry cartoons, what kind of creature is Tyke?
a) Cat
b) Dog
c) Fox
d) Wolf

15. Which comic-strip character lives in Bengalla?
a) Batman
b) Superman
c) Phantom
d) Shaktimaan

16. In the Asterix comics, who could make beautiful flowers grow in moments?
a) Getafix
b) Botanix
c) Prefix
d) Suffix

17. With which comic-strip character would you associate Gwen Stacy?
a) Spider-Man

b) Superman
c) Batman
d) Phantom

18. Morty and Ferdie are this famous cartoon character's nephews. Who is he?
a) Popeye
b) Donald Duck
c) Henry
d) Mickey Mouse

19. Which of these superheroes gets his powers from a ring?
a) Superman
b) Phantom
c) Batman
d) Green Lantern

20. I am a lazy fat cat who hates Mondays, loves lasagna and my owner is Jon Arbuckle. Which cartoon character am I?
a) Crookshanks
b) Garfield
c) Tom
d) Cheshire Cat

COMPUTERS

1. Which of these can you type using the letters in the first row of
    a standard computer keyboard?
    a) EUROPE
    b) ASIA
    c) AFRICA
    d) NORTH AMERICA

2. Which of these words comes from the Latin word for 'runner'?
    a) Cursor
    b) Monitor
    c) Scanner
    d) Printer

3. Which of these computer languages was developed by John
    G. Kemeny and Thomas E. Kurtz?
    a) Ruby
    b) Java

c) C++

d) BASIC

4. Which of these combinations is used to save a document in Microsoft Word?

a) Ctrl + F

b) Ctrl + S

c) Ctrl + Alt

d) Ctrl + Del

5. Name the digital virtual assistant released by Microsoft in 2015 along with Windows 10.

a) Cortana

b) Alexa

c) Siri

d) Alpha

6. While working on a Windows computer, which key should you press along with the Ctrl key to close a spreadsheet?

a) W

b) O

c) S

d) C

7. The process of converting information or data into a code, especially to prevent unauthorized access, is known as . . .

a) Encryption

b) Reboot

c) Zip file

d) Spam

8. In a Word document, which key should you press along with the Ctrl key to undo the last action?
a) X
b) Y
c) R
d) Z

9. On a standard computer keyboard, which number appears on the key with '&'?
a) 5
b) 6
c) 7
d) 8

10. Which key appears between the Alt keys on a QWERTY keyboard?
a) Enter
b) Space bar
c) Tab
d) Shift

11. Which function key activates the Help menu on a standard computer keyboard?
a) F4
b) F3
c) F2
d) F1

12. Which of these is a fault in a computer program causing it to function in an unanticipated manner?
a) Bee

b) Bug
c) Slug
d) Leech

13. What is the sudden complete failure of a computer system or component called?
a) Crash
b) Audit
c) Blockage
d) Reboot

14. The speed of a computer mouse is measured in ...
a) Donalds
b) Mickeys
c) Bugs
d) Winnies

15. AZERTY and Dvorak are different layouts of ...
a) Keyboards
b) Monitors
c) Scanners
d) Microprocessors

16. Which search engine was initially named 'Jerry and David's Guide to the World Wide Web'?
a) AskMe
b) Bing
c) Google
d) Yahoo

17. Which of these is often regarded as the 'brain' of the computer?
a) CPU
b) Monitor
c) Mouse
d) Printer

18. Which of these is also the name of a programming language created by Guido van Rossum?
a) Cobra
b) Python
c) Mamba
d) Anaconda

19. Which programming language was created by John Backus in 1957?
a) FORTRAN
b) C
c) COBOL
d) ALGOL

20. Which of these is an output device?
a) Keyboard
b) Mouse
c) Printer
d) Joystick

CRICKET I

1. What was devised by two mathematicians, Frank and Tony, to help decide the result of one-day cricket matches when rain interrupts play?
   a) Duckworth-Lewis system
   b) Powerplay
   c) Hawk-Eye technology
   d) Third umpire

2. Who was the first Indian to score a century on his World Cup debut?
   a) Anil Kumble
   b) C.K. Nayudu
   c) Virat Kohli
   d) Suresh Raina

3. What does a cricket umpire signal by crossing and recrossing the wrists below his/her waist?
   a) Dead ball
   b) Six
   c) One run short
   d) Wide

4. Who wrote the book titled *The Jubilee Book of Cricket*?
   a) Ranjitsinhji
   b) Duleepsinhji
   c) C.K. Nayudu
   d) I.A.K. Pataudi

5. Who among these captained the winning team in the 2008 ICC Under-19 Cricket World Cup?
   a) Rohit Sharma
   b) Prithvi Shaw
   c) Virat Kohli
   d) Shikhar Dhawan

6. Who scored the first-ever Test century for India?
   a) C.K. Nayudu
   b) Lala Amarnath
   c) Vijay Hazare
   d) Polly Umrigar

7. In 2018, who became the first woman cricketer to take 200 wickets in ODIs?
   a) Harmanpreet Kaur
   b) Ekta Bisht

c) Shikha Pandey
d) Jhulan Goswami

8. Combining the Tests, ODIs and Twenty20s he played, which cricketer has made the most hundreds in his career?
a) Ricky Ponting
b) Jacques Kallis
c) Sachin Tendulkar
d) Brian Lara

9. A non-batsman promoted up the order towards the end of a day's play with the idea of shielding a recognized batsman in the final overs is a . . .
a) Chinaman
b) Nightwatchman
c) Mankad
d) Pinch hitter

10. Which IPL team has the Sudarshan Chakra in its logo?
a) Chennai Super Kings
b) Rajasthan Royals
c) Punjab Kings
d) Mumbai Indians

11. Who holds the record for the most runs scored in an innings in both Test (international) and first-class cricket?
a) Brian Lara
b) Donald Bradman
c) Garfield Sobers
d) Sunil Gavaskar

12. Against which team does Australia play the Ashes?
a) England
b) India
c) Bangladesh
d) Bhutan

13. Which wicketkeeper holds the Indian record for the most dismissals in his ODI career?
a) Rahul Dravid
b) Kiran More
c) Syed Kirmani
d) M.S. Dhoni

14. Traditionally, cricket bats are made from the wood of which tree?
a) Willow
b) Banyan
c) Eucalyptus
d) Pine

15. In cricketing slang, what is a golden duck?
a) When a batsman is out on a duck in the second innings of a Test
b) When a batsman is out on the first ball he faces
c) When a batsman scores zero in both innings of a Test
d) When a batsman remains unbeaten on zero

16. During the 2017 Women's Cricket World Cup, who surpassed Charlotte Edwards to become the highest run scorer in ODIs?
a) Mithali Raj
b) Smriti Mandhana

c) Punam Raut
d) Harleen Deol

17. Who was the first Indian cricketer to score five centuries in five consecutive Test matches?
a) Virender Sehwag
b) Gautam Gambhir
c) Sachin Tendulkar
d) Harbhajan Singh

18. In which city is M. Chinnaswamy stadium located?
a) Bengaluru
b) Chennai
c) Hyderabad
d) Cuttack

19. Who has captained India for the most number of ODIs?
a) Mohammad Azharuddin
b) Sourav Ganguly
c) M.S. Dhoni
d) Sachin Tendulkar

20. In 1997, who became the first living non-royal to appear on Australian stamps?
a) Allan Border
b) Donald Bradman
c) Dennis Lillee
d) Adam Gilchrist

CRICKET II

1. The Sawai Mansingh Stadium is the home ground of which IPL team?
    a) Mumbai Indians
    b) Rajasthan Royals
    c) Chennai Super Kings
    d) Punjab Kings

2. Which of these denotes fielding positions very close to the batsman?
    a) Silly point
    b) Stupid point
    c) Foolish point
    d) Idiot point

3. Who hit 158 runs off just 73 balls in the inaugural game of the IPL, becoming the first to score a 50, a 100 and also a 150 in the league?
a) Brendon McCullum
b) Glenn McGrath
c) Jacques Kallis
d) Ashley Noffke

4. Among left-handed batsmen, who has scored the most Test runs for India?
a) Ajit Wadekar
b) Yuvraj Singh
c) Ravi Shastri
d) Sourav Ganguly

5. After Sachin Tendulkar, who has scored the most runs in Test cricket?
a) Shivnarine Chanderpaul
b) Virender Sehwag
c) Ricky Ponting
d) Kumar Sangakkara

6. How many times has India won the ICC Cricket World Cup?
a) One
b) Two
c) Three
d) Six

7. In 2016, who became the youngest cricketer ever to score centuries against all Test-playing nations?
a) Kane Williamson

b) Ben Stokes
c) Steve Smith
d) Jason Holder

8. Fill in the blank to complete the name of an IPL team:
Sunrisers _____.
a) Bengaluru
b) Hyderabad
c) Chennai
d) Kolkata

9. In Twenty20 Internationals, who has hit the most number of sixes in his career?
a) Eoin Morgan
b) Chris Gayle
c) Martin Guptill
d) Rohit Sharma

10. Which cricketer has bowled the most number of balls in Twenty20 Internationals for India?
a) Jasprit Bumrah
b) Ravindra Jadeja
c) Ravichandran Ashwin
d) Yuzvendra Chahal

11. Which cricketer was nicknamed Jammy?
a) Syed Kirmani
b) Aravinda de Silva
c) Javagal Srinath
d) Rahul Dravid

12. In which 2011 film would you see former cricketers Andrew Symonds, Herschelle Gibbs and Nasser Hussain together?
a) *Lagaan*
b) *Band Baaja Baaraat*
c) *102 Not Out*
d) *Patiala House*

13. Who scored his first ODI hundred in his 79th match?
a) Sachin Tendulkar
b) Sourav Ganguly
c) Rahul Dravid
d) M.S. Dhoni

14. Who was the first cricketer to hit a six off the first ball of a Test match?
a) Shahid Afridi
b) Chris Gayle
c) AB de Villiers
d) Kevin Pietersen

15. Which cricketer is nicknamed Mr 360 or Superman?
a) AB de Villiers
b) Joe Root
c) Matthew Hayden
d) Ricky Ponting

16. Which of these was introduced in a Test match between Australia and New Zealand in 2015?
a) The pink ball
b) The Hawk-Eye

c) The vanishing spray
d) The LED wicket

17. Actor Saif Ali Khan's grandfather played Test cricket for . . .
a) India and England
b) India and Pakistan
c) Pakistan and England
d) Pakistan, England and India

18. *Straight from the Heart* is the autobiography of . . .
a) Sunil Gavaskar
b) Kapil Dev
c) Rahul Dravid
d) Sachin Tendulkar

19. Which cricket team is referred to as the Proteas?
a) West Indies
b) Australia
c) New Zealand
d) South Africa

20. What do umpires signal with a hand touching their raised knee?
a) Leg bye
b) No-ball
c) Wide
d) Dead ball

DISEASES AND DISORDERS

1. Whose work on the smallpox vaccine was inspired by Blossom the cow?
   a) Alexander Fleming
   b) Louis Pasteur
   c) Edward Jenner
   d) Alexander Graham Bell

2. Which is the most common infection among humans?
   a) Hepatitis B
   b) Eye infection
   c) Skin infection
   d) The common cold

3. Hepatic diseases are also called...
   a) Kidney diseases
   b) Heart diseases

c) Liver diseases
d) Lung diseases

4. In type 1 of which disease does the human body not make enough insulin?
a) Diabetes
b) Jaundice
c) Swine flu
d) Malaria

5. Uveitis is the inflammation of which organ of the human body?
a) Eyes
b) Liver
c) Brain
d) Lungs

6. According to the US National Library of Medicine, which is the second-most common disorder?
a) Tooth decay
b) Cataract
c) Pneumonia
d) Headache

7. Who would you consult if you were affected by caries?
a) Dermatologist
b) Pulmonologist
c) Dentist
d) Hepatologist

8. Lateral epicondylitis is better known to us by what name?
a) Tennis elbow
b) Tennis finger
c) Tennis foot
d) Tennis ear

9. Which disease is also known as hydrophobia?
a) Jaundice
b) Rabies
c) Dengue
d) Typhoid

10. The functioning of which organ in the human body is tested by a laboratory procedure known as LFT?
a) Lungs
b) Brain
c) Liver
d) Kidneys

11. Dermatology deals with the treatment of disorders related to ...
a) Skin
b) Heart
c) Eyes
d) Kidneys

12. Parkinson's disease is a progressive disorder of the ...
a) Digestive system
b) Circulatory system
c) Urinary system
d) Nervous system

13. With which part of the human body is prickly heat associated?
   a) Hair
   b) Skin
   c) Tongue
   d) Nails

14. Coronary arteries supply blood to the muscles of the . . .
   a) Ears
   b) Heart
   c) Kidneys
   d) Small intestine

15. MMR is a safe combination vaccine that protects against measles, rubella and . . .
   a) Mumps
   b) Malaria
   c) Muscular dystrophy
   d) Meningitis

16. A1C is a laboratory test that shows the average level of _____ over the previous three months. Fill in the blank.
   a) Protein
   b) Creatinine
   c) Urea
   d) Blood sugar

17. Which of these diseases was first identified during an outbreak in southern Tanzania in 1952?
   a) Dengue
   b) Chikungunya

c) Encephalitis
d) Bird flu

18. Which of these words can be used to describe a large waterfall as well as a medical condition affecting the eyes?
a) Cataract
b) Glaucoma
c) Conjunctivitis
d) Gout

19. Arrhythmia is a disorder of which part of the human body?
a) Liver
b) Heart
c) Kidneys
d) Lungs

20. A gastroenterologist specializes in treating diseases of the . . .
a) Nerves
b) Blood
c) Ankles and feet
d) Stomach

ECONOMY

1. According to reports published in 2007, over 20 per cent of the decorative gold used throughout the world was used in . . .
   a) Indian saris
   b) Minting coins
   c) Pasta
   d) Tooth fillings

2. Who were the first to use paper money?
   a) The Chinese
   b) The Greeks
   c) The Mexicans
   d) The Egyptians

3. Bolivar is the basic monetary unit of . . .
   a) Germany
   b) Italy

c) Thailand
d) Venezuela

4. Which princely state issued currency called the Osmania Sicca?
a) Hyderabad
b) Patiala
c) Gwalior
d) Bhopal

5. Who initiated the import of silk cocoons from China to encourage silk rearing in Mysore (now Mysuru)?
a) Rajaraja Chola
b) Krishnadevaraya
c) Tipu Sultan
d) Shah Jahan

6. In 1992, who became the first living person to appear on the banknote of New Zealand?
a) Edmund Hillary
b) Richard Hadlee
c) Ernest Rutherford
d) Peter Jackson

7. Which word, introduced by Sher Shah Suri, was used for a gold coin weighing 169 grains?
a) Dam
b) Rupiya
c) Mohur
d) Tanka

8. Which country is the largest producer of mangoes in the world?
a) India
b) Pakistan
c) China
d) South Africa

9. In 1903–04, what appeared on the first machine-struck coins of Hyderabad?
a) Salar Jung Museum
b) Charminar
c) Falaknuma Palace
d) A pearl

10. What was the first item from Assam to obtain the geographical indications tag?
a) Bhut Jolokia chillies
b) Joha rice
c) Assam tea
d) Muga silk

11. Around AD 1777, Nanakshahis were made in Amritsar. What were these?
a) Bank drafts
b) Coins
c) Deposit slips
d) Chequebooks

12. Who was the union finance minister from 1982–1984?
a) P. Chidambaram
b) Yashwant Sinha

c) Manmohan Singh
d) Pranab Mukherjee

13. In 2016, which country bought more gold jewellery than India and the United States combined?
a) China
b) Egypt
c) Turkey
d) Saudi Arabia

14. The rupee is the currency of which of these countries?
a) Bhutan
b) Myanmar
c) Afghanistan
d) Mauritius

15. Which of these notable women was the first to present the Union Budget of India?
a) Nirmala Sitharaman
b) Indira Gandhi
c) Sushma Swaraj
d) Sonia Gandhi

16. The Cavendish variety of which fruit accounts for around 47 per cent of global production?
a) Apple
b) Banana
c) Mango
d) Orange

17. Which ruler introduced copper coins with Gurmukhi legends?
a) Chandragupta I
b) Prithviraj Chauhan
c) Maharana Pratap
d) Ranjit Singh

18. The session of Parliament from February to April/May is called . . .
a) Budget session
b) Business session
c) Money Bill session
d) Joint session

19. In India, the first design of what was attempted by Col. William Forbes of the Calcutta Mint (now India Government Mint)?
a) The one-rupee note
b) The national symbol
c) The postage stamp
d) The national flag

20. The bulk of the silk produced in the world is of which variety?
a) Eri
b) Tussar
c) Mulberry
d) Muga

ENTERTAINMENT

1. *The Last Lear* was the first English-language film of which of these actors?
    a) Amitabh Bachchan
    b) Irrfan Khan
    c) Naseeruddin Shah
    d) Om Puri

2. The 2012 film *Nanban* is the south Indian remake of which Hindi film?
    a) *Dil Chahta Hai*
    b) *Zindagi Na Milegi Dobara*
    c) *3 Idiots*
    d) *Wanted*

3. Which film connects Meena Kumari, Moushumi Chatterjee and Vidya Balan?
    a) *Devdas*

b) *Balika Badhu*
c) *Dil Chahta Hai*
d) *Parineeta*

4. The name of which Akshay Kumar film was taken from a tag line behind a truck?
   a) *Khiladi*
   b) *Singh Is Kinng*
   c) *Dabangg*
   d) *Khatta Meetha*

5. In the film *Jodhaa Akbar*, if Hrithik Roshan was Akbar, who played the role of Jodha?
   a) Rani Mukherji
   b) Aishwarya Rai
   c) Katrina Kaif
   d) Deepika Padukone

6. Where is Ramoji Film City located?
   a) Bengaluru
   b) Cuttack
   c) Hyderabad
   d) Thiruvananthapuram

7. *Rockstar* was the last released film of which legendary actor?
   a) Raj Kapoor
   b) Shammi Kapoor
   c) Sunil Dutt
   d) Dev Anand

8. Who played the role of the young Sunny Deol in the 1983 film *Betaab*?
   a) Sonu Nigam
   b) Jugal Hansraj
   c) Hrithik Roshan
   d) Ranbir Kapoor

9. Which historical character did Ranveer Singh play in a 2015 film co-starring Priyanka Chopra?
   a) Ashoka
   b) Peshwa Bajirao
   c) Akbar
   d) Alexander

10. Rajiv Hari Om Bhatia was a martial arts instructor before he changed his profession. How is he better known?
   a) Akshay Kumar
   b) Tiger Shroff
   c) Sunny Deol
   d) Varun Dhawan

11. 'Abdul Rashid Salim' are a part of which actor's full name?
   a) Aamir Khan
   b) Shah Rukh Khan
   c) Irrfan Khan
   d) Salman Khan

12. Who returned to the silver screen after fourteen years with the film *English Vinglish*?
   a) Karisma Kapoor
   b) Sridevi

c) Juhi Chawla
d) Madhuri Dixit

13. Which of these actresses made her debut with Salman Khan?
a) Anushka Sharma
b) Deepika Padukone
c) Nargis Fakhri
d) Sonakshi Sinha

14. Who was the director of the 2013 film *Vishwaroopam*?
a) Prakash Raj
b) Rohit Shetty
c) Rajnikanth
d) Kamal Haasan

15. Published in a school textbook, the chapter titled *From Bus Conductor to Superstar*, is based on whose life?
a) M.G. Ramachandran
b) Rajinikanth
c) M.S. Swaminathan
d) Gundappa Viswanath

16. Who composed the music for the Hollywood film *127 Hours*?
a) Ilaiyaraaja
b) Pritam
c) A.R. Rahman
d) Jay-Z

17. The KiLiKi language, which initally had 750 words and forty rules of grammar, was created for which film?
a) *The Lord of the Rings*

b) *Avatar*
c) *Bajrangi Bhaijaan*
d) *Baahubali: The Beginning*

18. The Force Awakens is a part of which film series?
a) Star Wars
b) Avengers
c) Harry Potter
d) Mission Impossible

19. In which of these films did Irrfan Khan not appear?
a) *Jurassic World*
b) *Life of Pi*
c) *Slumdog Millionaire*
d) *The Great Gatsby*

20. Which of these greetings is also the name of a 2014 film directed by Farah Khan?
a) Merry Christmas
b) Happy New Year
c) Happy Birthday
d) Bon Voyage!

ENVIRONMENT

1. In 1971, which organization was founded to oppose US nuclear testing at Amchitka Island?
   a) World Wildlife Fund
   b) Greenpeace
   c) Friends of Nature
   d) World Nature Organization

2. The secretariat of the Intergovernmental Panel on Climate Change is located in . . .
   a) Amsterdam
   b) Geneva
   c) The Hague
   d) New York City

3. The law of which country states that it shall maintain at least 60 per cent of its forest cover at all times?
   a) Myanmar

b) Bhutan
c) Sri Lanka
d) Bangladesh

4. If 'N' stands for Natural and 'G' stands for Gas, what does 'C' in CNG stand for?
   a) Carbonated
   b) Cycled
   c) Compressed
   d) Crystallized

5. In Kannada, the word 'Appiko' in the Appiko Movement means to . . .
   a) Embrace
   b) Cut
   c) Pray
   d) Paint

6. The name of which of these comes from the Japanese words for 'harbour' and 'wave'?
   a) Earthquake
   b) Tsunami
   c) Typhoon
   d) Cyclone

7. The United Nations observes 22 April as International . . .
   a) Mother Earth Day
   b) Wildlife Day
   c) Malaria Day
   d) Day of Parents

8. When is World Environment Day observed by the United Nations?
   a) 5 June
   b) 31 May
   c) 1 April
   d) 14 November

9. The mission of the Ramsar Convention is the conservation and wise use of all . . .
   a) Wetlands
   b) Deserts
   c) Ocean currents
   d) Gases

10. Who among these wrote *Silent Spring*, a book on environmental pollution?
   a) Jane Goodall
   b) David Attenborough
   c) Rachel Carson
   d) Medha Patkar

11. Which film, set in AD 2805, is about a robot who needs to clean up the garbage on Earth?
   a) *Shrek*
   b) *Ice Age*
   c) *Minions*
   d) *WALL-E*

12. If 'C' stands for Compact and 'L' stands for Lamp, what does 'F' in CFL stand for?
   a) Filament

b) Fluorine
c) Fluorescent
d) Fragile

13. Which was the first carbon-negative country in the world?
a) Nepal
b) Bhutan
c) Cambodia
d) China

14. According to Sunderlal Bahuguna, 'Ecology is permanent _____.' Fill in the blank.
a) Economy
b) Science
c) Happiness
d) Life

15. The name of which national park literally means 'ten villages'?
a) Sariska
b) Dachigam
c) Sundarbans
d) Anamudi Shola

16. Which region is sometimes referred to as 'the lungs of the earth'?
a) The Himalayas
b) The Amazon rainforest
c) Yellowstone National Park
d) The Great Barrier Reef

17. Who fought against an energy corporation in the 2000 film *Erin Brockovich*?
a) Julia Roberts
b) Demi Moore
c) Meryl Streep
d) Holly Hunter

18. Who was the project manager of the Global Precipitation Measurement project at NASA in *Swades*?
a) Salman Khan
b) Shah Rukh Khan
c) Aamir Khan
d) Saif Ali Khan

19. What would you call the phenomenon that results in reduced visibility due to the scattering of light caused by aerosols?
a) Haze
b) Fog
c) Insolation
d) Smoke

20. The World Day to Combat _____ and Drought is observed on 17 June by the United Nations. Fill in the blank.
a) Deforestation
b) Smog
c) Desertification
d) Famine

FAMOUS WOMEN

1. Who was the first Indian classical musician to perform at the UN General Assembly?
   a) M.S. Subbulakshmi
   b) Mother Teresa
   c) Lata Mangeshkar
   d) Shubha Mudgal

2. *Raseedi Ticket* is the autobiography of which author?
   a) Mahasweta Devi
   b) Amrita Pritam
   c) Mahadevi Verma
   d) Ashapurna Devi

3. Who was the first Indian woman to win an Olympic medal?
   a) Sania Mirza
   b) Karnam Malleswari

c) Sakshi Malik
d) M.C. Mary Kom

4. On whose life is the documentary *Yes Madam, Sir* based?
   a) Indira Gandhi
   b) Kiran Bedi
   c) Sushma Swaraj
   d) Sheila Dikshit

5. In 1996, who became the fourth honorary citizen of the United States?
   a) Aung San Suu Kyi
   b) Mother Teresa
   c) Rigoberta Menchú Tum
   d) Jane Goodall

6. Who was the first woman to win the Bharat Ratna?
   a) Indira Gandhi
   b) Aruna Asaf Ali
   c) Asha Bhosle
   d) M.S. Subbulakshmi

7. Which of these actresses is a former Miss World?
   a) Anushka Sharma
   b) Aishwarya Rai
   c) Sushmita Sen
   d) Katrina Kaif

8. Which feat did Arati Saha achieve in 1959?
   a) She swam across the English Channel.
   b) She climbed Mount Everest.

c) She reached the South Pole.

d) She set foot on the moon.

9. Which Mughal empress had coins minted in her name?

a) Jodha Bai

b) Nur Jahan

c) Mumtaz Mahal

d) Jahanara Begum

10. Which famous person's life forms the central plot of the novel, *Queen of Glory*?

a) Shahnaz Husain

b) Rani Lakshmibai

c) Gayatri Devi

d) Chand Bibi

11. Which famous ruler's tomb lies at Mohalla Bulbuli Khana in Old Delhi?

a) Razia Sultan

b) Mumtaz Mahal

c) Nur Jahan

d) Rani Lakshmibai

12. Which famous lady wrote the book *Figuring: The Joy of Numbers*?

a) Arundhati Roy

b) Shakuntala Devi

c) Sonia Gandhi

d) Mother Teresa

13. In 2011, who became the chief minister of Tamil Nadu?
   a) Sushma Swaraj
   b) Sheila Dikshit
   c) Mayawati
   d) J. Jayalalithaa

14. In 2008, who received the first copy of the e-Passport in India?
   a) Priyanka Chopra
   b) Pratibha Patil
   c) Sonia Gandhi
   d) Lata Mangeshkar

15. German supporters of Angela Merkel call her 'Mutti', which means . . .
   a) Sister
   b) Mother
   c) Aunt
   d) Grandmother

16. Who was the first Indian woman ambassador to the USSR?
   a) Indira Gandhi
   b) Sarojini Naidu
   c) Annie Besant
   d) Vijaya Lakshmi Pandit

17. Which sportsperson is nicknamed 'Payyoli Express'?
   a) P.T. Usha
   b) Sania Mirza
   c) Saina Nehwal
   d) M.C. Mary Kom

18. Pratibha Patil, Margaret Alva and Vijaya Lakshmi Pandit had something in common. They were ...
a) Speakers of Lok Sabha
b) Chief ministers
c) Governors of RBI
d) Governors of Indian states

19. Who wrote the poem titled 'Blessings to Nivedita'?
a) Swami Vivekananda
b) Mahatma Gandhi
c) Jawaharlal Nehru
d) Rajendra Prasad

20. On 16 May 1920, who was recognized as a saint by the Roman Catholic Church?
a) Florence Nightingale
b) Mother Teresa
c) Joan of Arc
d) Jane Austen

FESTIVALS, FAIRS AND IMPORTANT DAYS

1. Dhanteras marks the beginning of which festival?
   a) Holi
   b) Diwali
   c) Guru Purnima
   d) Ganesh Chaturthi

2. Which of these festivals is held in Kisama, about 12 km from Kohima?
   a) Hornbill Festival
   b) Bohag Bihu
   c) Nishagandhi Nritya Utsav
   d) International Kite Festival

3. In Jainism, which festival commemorates Mahavira's attainment of moksha or salvation?
a) Diwali
b) Holi
c) Vasant Panchami
d) Raksha Bandhan

4. Chapchar Kut is an important spring festival of . . .
a) Odisha
b) Mizoram
c) Tamil Nadu
d) Haryana

5. The writer Washington Irving was the first person to describe that Father Christmas or Santa Claus . . .
a) Wears a red outfit
b) Slides down chimneys
c) Owns Rudolph the Red-Nosed Reindeer
d) Lives in London

6. The Kumbh Mela is held at the confluence of three rivers: Ganga, Yamuna and the mythical . . .
a) Saraswati
b) Narmada
c) Krishna
d) Kaveri

7. In which state is the Nagaur Fair held?
a) Rajasthan
b) Gujarat

c) Punjab

d) Haryana

8. Whose birth anniversary is celebrated as the International Day of Non-Violence by the United Nations?

a) Mahatma Gandhi

b) Adolf Hitler

c) Nelson Mandela

d) Mother Teresa

9. Janmashtami marks the birth anniversary of . . .

a) Ganesha

b) Krishna

c) Shiva

d) Indra

10. In which state of India is the Rann Festival held?

a) Maharashtra

b) Gujarat

c) Madhya Pradesh

d) Arunachal Pradesh

11. In which month is Hindi Diwas celebrated in India?

a) March

b) September

c) October

d) December

12. Who was born to destroy Mathura's demon king Kansa?

a) Rama

b) Krishna

c) Indra

d) Bharat

13. Whose birth anniversary is celebrated as National Youth Day in India?
   a) Swami Vivekananda
   b) Dhyan Chand
   c) Subhas Chandra Bose
   d) Bhagat Singh

14. Which festival commemorates Lord Rama's return to his kingdom Ayodhya after completing his fourteen-year exile?
   a) Holi
   b) Diwali
   c) Ganesh Chaturthi
   d) Pongal

15. Who was born in 1469 at Talwandi, near Lahore?
   a) Guru Arjan Dev
   b) Guru Nanak Dev
   c) Guru Gobind Singh
   d) Guru Amar Das

16. Which festival celebrates the golden reign of King Mahabali?
   a) Lohri
   b) Onam
   c) Gudi Padwa
   d) Chhath

17. Which of these fairs is held in Rajasthan?
   a) Pushkar Camel Fair

b) Sonepur Mela
c) Hemis Gompa Fair
d) Chandrabhaga Mela

18. Vasant Panchami is celebrated in honour of . . .
a) Saraswati
b) Lakshmi
c) Kali
d) Sita

19. Who among these prime ministers of India was born on Christmas Day?
a) V.P. Singh
b) Atal Bihari Vajpayee
c) Rajiv Gandhi
d) Indira Gandhi

20. Vesak commemorates the birth of . . .
a) Mahavira
b) Buddha
c) Krishna
d) Rama

FOOD I

1. Which spice is also known as mitha jira in Bengali?
   a) Celery
   b) Aniseed
   c) Fennel
   d) Cinnamon

2. The tomato was introduced to Europe by the . . .
   a) Germans
   b) Spanish
   c) French
   d) Greeks

3. Clementine and tangerine are varieties of which fruit?
   a) Apple
   b) Orange
   c) Guava
   d) Banana

4. The name of which vegetable comes from an Old French word meaning 'head'?
a) Brinjal
b) Cabbage
c) Bottle gourd
d) Pumpkin

5. The recipe of jahangiri, a sweet, is believed to be listed in Al Baghdadi's cookery book of the thirteenth century. How is it better known to us?
a) Kulfi
b) Jalebi
c) Gulab jamun
d) Barfi

6. Kufri Chandramukhi, Kufri Jyoti, Kufri Badshah, Kufri Sindhuri, Kufri Lalima are the main varieties of which crop grown in India?
a) Wheat
b) Apple
c) Potato
d) Rice

7. Which spice, known as zanjabil in Arabic, is the dried underground stem of a herbaceous tropical plant?
a) Garlic
b) Ginger
c) Chilli
d) Coriander

8. With which state would you associate dal baati choorma?
   a) Gujarat
   b) Rajasthan
   c) Tamil Nadu
   d) Uttar Pradesh

9. Which of these is a ball of deep-fried paneer or khoya boiled in sugar syrup?
   a) Gajar halwa
   b) Gulab jamun
   c) Shrikhand
   d) Kulfi

10. Traditionally, what is the main component of gatte in the dish gatte ki sabzi?
   a) Besan
   b) Paneer
   c) Aloo
   d) Rajma

11. What are oolong, green and black varieties of?
   a) Coffee
   b) Cocoa beans
   c) Tea
   d) Dates

12. Grown only at Alirajpur in Madhya Pradesh, what is Noor Jahan a variety of?
   a) Orange
   b) Apple

c) Mango

d) Banana

13. Lasagna is a type of ...
   a) Pickle
   b) Pasta
   c) Salad
   d) Pizza

14. In which of these places did the dish momo originate?
   a) Tibet
   b) South Korea
   c) Vietnam
   d) Jordan

15. Ranbir, Taraori, Kasturi and Mahi Sugandha are types of ...
   a) Basmati rice
   b) Darjeeling tea
   c) Rasgullas
   d) Motichoor laddoos

16. The name of which of these food items means 'stir-fried noodles' in Chinese?
   a) Chow mein
   b) Mei fun
   c) Chop suey
   d) Dim sum

17. Which of these states is famous for litti chokha?
   a) Bihar
   b) Maharashtra

c) Kerala

d) Tamil Nadu

18. Which spice is called zafran in Urdu?
a) Saffron
b) Turmeric
c) Ginger
d) Garlic

19. Hilsa is the national fish of which neighbouring country of India?
a) Bangladesh
b) Sri Lanka
c) Nepal
d) Pakistan

20. What is an elaborate Kashmiri meal, traditionally consisting of thirty-six dishes, called?
a) Dastarkhwan
b) Mezbaan
c) Wazwan
d) Makaan

FOOD II

1. Which of these is a popular Tibetan noodle soup?
   a) Dhokla
   b) Upma
   c) Idli
   d) Thukpa

2. The colour of the clothing of the Capuchin monks lends its name to a type of . . .
   a) Cake
   b) Coffee
   c) Biscuit
   d) Pizza

3. Which of these sweets is also the name of a film directed by Anurag Basu?
   a) Rasgulla
   b) Laddoo

    c) Barfi
    d) Sandesh

4. Gelato is mainly a variety of . . .
    a) Pizza
    b) Pasta
    c) Ice cream
    d) Burger

5. Which of these is served as sliced meat roasted on a spit?
    a) Falafel
    b) Shawarma
    c) Hummus
    d) Keema

6. Raisins are partially dried forms of which of these?
    a) Oranges
    b) Dates
    c) Grapes
    d) Cherries

7. The famous layered dessert bebinca, made of flour, coconut milk and eggs in a clay oven, is a speciality of . . .
    a) Goa
    b) Karnataka
    c) Nagaland
    d) Punjab

8. What is the colour of the circle on the symbol for vegetarian food on food packets?
    a) Brown

b) White
c) Green
d) Blue

9. The name of which fruit comes from the Latin words meaning 'apple having many seeds'?
   a) Litchi
   b) Banana
   c) Orange
   d) Pomegranate

10. What is the most common method of preparing potatoes across the world?
   a) Boiling
   b) Deep-frying
   c) Pickling
   d) Baking

11. The Aztecs gave a name meaning 'bitter water' to it and they mixed vanilla and chillies to it for flavour. What is it?
   a) Coffee
   b) Chocolate
   c) Tea
   d) Lemonade

12. The name of which of these comes from an Arabic word meaning 'that which prevents sleep'?
   a) Coffee
   b) Tea
   c) Ice cream
   d) Chocolate

13. In India, *Citrus reticulata* is the most important commercial species of ...
a) Apple
b) Mango
c) Banana
d) Orange

14. In 2011, which food was named the world's most popular dish in a survey conducted by the charity Oxfam?
a) Sandwich
b) Biscuit
c) Pasta
d) Pizza

15. What is the main ingredient of rogan josh?
a) Egg
b) Meat
c) Paneer
d) Mushroom

16. *Solanum tuberosum* is the scientific name of ...
a) Carrot
b) Tomato
c) Potato
d) Brinjal

17. Which spice is also known as yellow ginger?
a) Fennel
b) Turmeric
c) Cardamom
d) Clove

18. Which of these food items is said to have been created by Ashok Vaidya in Mumbai?
a) Lal maans
b) Mysore pak
c) Petha
d) Vada pav

19. What was Chhota Bheem's favourite sweet?
a) Laddoo
b) Barfi
c) Jalebi
d) Rasgulla

20. Who is regarded as the 'father of White Revolution' in India?
a) Sundarlal Bahuguna
b) Baba Amte
c) Verghese Kurien
d) M.S. Swaminathan

GEOGRAPHY OF INDIA

1. Which of these states lies on the eastern coast of India?
a) Uttar Pradesh
b) Gujarat
c) West Bengal
d) Maharashtra

2. Which Indian river was referred to as Shatadru in Sanskrit?
a) Saraswati
b) Beas
c) Chenab
d) Sutlej

3. Where would you come across islands named Landfall Island, Interview Island, Ritchie's Archipelago and Rutland Island?
a) Puducherry
b) Andaman and Nicobar Islands

c) Lakshadweep
d) Maharashtra

4. Which is the largest state in the north-eastern region of India in terms of area?
   a) Arunachal Pradesh
   b) Tripura
   c) Assam
   d) Meghalaya

5. Khardung La, Zoji La and Jelep La are names of different . . .
   a) Lakes in Goa
   b) Mountain passes
   c) Deserts in Rajasthan
   d) Districts of Kerala

6. Which port city is also home to the Eastern Naval Command of the Indian Navy?
   a) Visakhapatnam
   b) Kandla
   c) Kolkata
   d) Mangaluru

7. Which of these rivers originates in India?
   a) Tigris
   b) Brahmaputra
   c) Huang Ho
   d) Mahanadi

8. Rampur, Sitapur and Chitrakoot are districts of which state of India?
a) Karnataka
b) Rajasthan
c) Kerala
d) Uttar Pradesh

9. Which part of the human body does the hill station Nainital gets its name from?
a) Ears
b) Eyes
c) Lips
d) Feet

10. Which river's tributaries are Jhelum, Chenab and Ravi?
a) Indus
b) Ganga
c) Brahmaputra
d) Krishna

11. Which of these states is landlocked?
a) Bihar
b) Odisha
c) Maharashtra
d) Karnataka

12. In honour of which mountain is the Pang Lhabsol Festival celebrated in Sikkim?
a) Anamudi
b) Kanchenjunga

c) Lhotse
d) Mount Everest

13. The Kathiawar peninsula is a part of which state in India?
    a) Tamil Nadu
    b) Kerala
    c) Gujarat
    d) Madhya Pradesh

14. Yanam, Mahe and Karaikal are parts of which union territory?
    a) Chandigarh
    b) Lakshadweep
    c) Puducherry
    d) Andaman and Nicobar Islands

15. Over which river is the Bhakra-Nangal Dam built?
    a) Sutlej
    b) Kaveri
    c) Tapti
    d) Krishna

16. Vagator, Arambol and Morjim are beaches located in which state of India?
    a) Maharashtra
    b) Goa
    c) Tamil Nadu
    d) Kerala

17. Which city in Uttarakhand is also known as Mayapuri, Kapila and Gangadwar?
    a) Almora

b) Haridwar
c) Dehradun
d) Chamoli

18. More than 70 km long, what is sometimes referred to as the 'white snake'?
a) The Ganges
b) Khyber Pass
c) The Siachen Glacier
d) Nilgiri Hills

19. Which of these states does not share its border with Bangladesh?
a) Tripura
b) Meghalaya
c) Nagaland
d) Mizoram

20. Which mountain peak was referred to as Peak XV before 1865?
a) K2
b) Mount Everest
c) Lhotse
d) Nanda Devi

GREET RULERS

1. Who among these was not a Navratna in Akbar's court?
   a) Todar Mal
   b) Abul Fazl
   c) Faizi
   d) Bairam Khan

2. Fill in the blank to complete the name of Shahab-ud-din Muhammad _____, a Mughal emperor born in 1592.
   a) Humayun
   b) Akbar
   c) Jahangir
   d) Shah Jahan

3. Which king sent officers known as Dhamma Mahamattas to promote dharma throughout his empire?
   a) Ashoka
   b) Samudragupta

c) Prithviraj Chauhan
d) Rajaraja Chola

4. Which famous person was born at the Shivneri hill fort?
a) Tipu Sultan
b) Shivaji
c) Aurangzeb
d) Babur

5. Brihadratha was the last ruler of which empire?
a) Maratha Empire
b) Mongol Empire
c) Mughal Empire
d) Mauryan Empire

6. Who among these was a descendant of Timur and Genghis Khan?
a) Sher Shah Suri
b) Babur
c) Tipu Sultan
d) Iltutmish

7. Which great Maratha warrior set up a council of eight ministers known as Ashta Pradhan?
a) Aurangzeb
b) Shivaji
c) Nadir Shah
d) Tantia Tope

8. In 326 BC, who defeated Porus in the Battle of the Hydaspes (now Jhelum)?
   a) Alexander the Great
   b) Napoleon
   c) Mahmud of Ghazni
   d) Timur

9. What title was given to the chief minister in Shivaji's council of ministers?
   a) Peshwa
   b) Alamgir
   c) Chhatrapati
   d) Maharana

10. Which religion did Ashoka convert to towards the later part of his life?
    a) Buddhism
    b) Jainism
    c) Sikhism
    d) Baha'ism

11. Which ruler of the Delhi Sultanate was a slave of Muhammad Ghori?
    a) Qutbuddin Aibak
    b) Muhammad bin Tughluq
    c) Balban
    d) Razia Sultan

12. Who was the last Tirthankara of Jainism?
    a) Sathya Sai Baba
    b) Buddha

c) Guru Nanak

d) Mahavira

13. Siri, one of the seven cities of Delhi, was built by which ruler?

a) Iltutmish

b) Muhammad bin Tughluq

c) Firuz Tughluq

d) Alauddin Khilji

14. Asvaghosa was the spiritual counsellor of which king?

a) Kanishka

b) Harshavardhana

c) Ashoka

d) Chandragupta

15. In 1576, the Battle of Haldighati was fought between Raja Man Singh of Amber, the general of the Mughal emperor Akbar, and . . .

a) Maharana Pratap Singh of Mewar

b) Kanishka

c) Samudragupta

d) Ashoka

16. Who among these was a ruler of the Slave dynasty?

a) Akbar

b) Babur

c) Sher Shah Suri

d) Iltutmish

17. Which Mughal emperor was Shah Jahan's grandfather?

a) Aurangzeb

b) Jahangir
c) Akbar
d) Babur

18. Whose daughter was Gulbadan Begum, the author of *Humayun-Nama*?
a) Babur
b) Akbar
c) Humayun
d) Jahangir

19. Which city was founded by the fifth king of the Qutb Shahi dynasty?
a) Bengaluru
b) Hyderabad
c) Lucknow
d) Ajmer

20. According to a letter by Maharaja Ranjit Singh, what did he wish to offer to Lord Jagannath?
a) Patiala fort
b) The river Sutlej
c) His turban
d) The Kohinoor

HINDI FILMS

1. Which actor's screen name was Vijay in more than twenty Hindi films?
   a) Rishi Kapoor
   b) Amitabh Bachchan
   c) Dharmendra
   d) Hrithik Roshan

2. Who was the director of the 2014 film *PK*?
   a) Aamir Khan
   b) Rajkumar Hirani
   c) Prabhu Deva
   d) Dibakar Banerjee

3. The 2007 film *Guru* is loosely based on the life of . . .
   a) Shah Rukh Khan
   b) Dhirubhai Ambani

c) Rabindranath Tagore
d) Dilip Kumar

4. Which director's first Hindi feature film was *Shatranj Ke Khilari?*
   a) Bimal Roy
   b) Satyajit Ray
   c) Mrinal Sen
   d) Guru Dutt

5. Which famous Hindi film actor is the grandson of the well-known Urdu poet Harivansh Rai Shrivastav?
   a) Amitabh Bachchan
   b) Shah Rukh Khan
   c) Saif Ali Khan
   d) Abhishek Bachchan

6. Who played the female lead in the films *Delhi-6, Aisha* and *Saawariya?*
   a) Sonam Kapoor
   b) Deepika Padukone
   c) Priyanka Chopra
   d) Amrita Rao

7. Who played the role of Milkha Singh in the film *Bhaag Milkha Bhaag?*
   a) Ranbir Kapoor
   b) Farhan Akhtar
   c) Hrithik Roshan
   d) Arjun Kapoor

8. Which actor won the National Film Award for Best Actor for the film *Shahid*?
a) Amit Sadh
b) Rajkummar Rao
c) Varun Dhawan
d) Sidharth Malhotra

9. What is the name of the witch in the film *Chhota Bheem and the Throne of Bali*?
a) Indumati
b) Rangda
c) Tuntun
d) Meena

10. Which film was released as *Shuai Jiao Baba*, translating as 'Let's Wrestle, Dad' in China?
a) *Sultan*
b) *Dangal*
c) *Taare Zameen Par*
d) *Secret Superstar*

11. Who made his directorial debut with *Dilwale Dulhania Le Jayenge*?
a) Aditya Chopra
b) Karan Johar
c) Anurag Kashyap
d) Anurag Basu

12. Which popular film's name was suggested by Salman Khan?
a) *Dilwale Dulhania Le Jayenge*
b) *Ra.One*

c) *Taare Zameen Par*
d) *Kai Po Che!*

13. Who directed the 2011 film *Zindagi Na Milegi Dobara*?
a) Nandita Das
b) Zoya Akhtar
c) Meghna Gulzar
d) Pooja Bhatt

14. Which of these films did not feature a real-life father-son as reel father-son in the film?
a) *Yamla Pagla Deewana*
b) *Sarkar*
c) *Munnabhai M.B.B.S.*
d) *Bunty Aur Babli*

15. The 2004 film *Main Hoon Na* marked the directorial debut of . . .
a) Sujoy Ghosh
b) Vishal Bhardwaj
c) Anurag Kashyap
d) Farah Khan

16. Who is the son of popular actress Neetu Singh?
a) Ranbir Kapoor
b) Arjun Kapoor
c) Shahid Kapoor
d) Aditya Roy Kapur

17. Among these actors, which one has represented India in rugby for almost twenty-five years?
a) Aamir Khan
b) Rahul Bose
c) Farhan Akhtar
d) Abhishek Bachchan

18. Which was Salman Khan and Katrina Kaif's first film together?
a) *Maine Pyaar Kyun Kiya*
b) *Ek Tha Tiger*
c) *Tiger Zinda Hai*
d) *Bharat*

19. Who among these played a double role in her first Hindi film?
a) Sonakshi Sinha
b) Deepika Padukone
c) Sonam Kapoor
d) Alia Bhatt

20. With which film did Farhan Akhtar make his debut as a director?
a) *Lakshya*
b) *Dil Chahta Hai*
c) *Don 2*
d) *Rock On!!*

HINDU MYTHOLOGY

1. What did Brahma create from Agni, Vayu and Ravi?
   a) The first three Vedas
   b) Tripura
   c) Shiva's trishul
   d) Saraswati, Lakshmi and Kali

2. Who constructed the city of Lanka?
   a) Vishwakarma
   b) Sushruta
   c) Dhanvantari
   d) Narada

3. According to the Mahabharata, who among these was Shakuni's sister?
   a) Uttara
   b) Draupadi

    c) Gandhari

    d) Kunti

4. From which part of Brahma's body was sage Narada born?
   a) Ears
   b) Toes
   c) Thumbs
   d) Lap

5. Who was also known as Dasanana as he had ten faces?
   a) Rama
   b) Hanuman
   c) Ravana
   d) Garuda

6. In the Ramayana, who is known as Pavanputra?
   a) Lakshmana
   b) Hanuman
   c) Janaka
   d) Vibhishana

7. Who among these had the most number of brothers?
   a) Lakshmana
   b) Bhima
   c) Duryodhana
   d) Nakula

8. Which modern-day city in India was known as Indraprastha, where the Pandavas lived?
   a) Kolkata
   b) Mumbai

c) New Delhi
d) Hyderabad

9. In the Ramayana, whose name literally means 'furrow', as she was found by her father while he was ploughing the field?
   a) Urmila
   b) Sita
   c) Mandodari
   d) Mandavi

10. The spots on the peacock's tail symbolize the ...
    a) Eyes of the gods
    b) Shiva's trishul
    c) Krishna's footprints
    d) Hanuman's teardrops

11. Who was the daughter of Viswamitra and Menaka?
    a) Aditi
    b) Ahalya
    c) Shakuntala
    d) Urmila

12. In the Ramayana, what was the capital of Dasharatha's kingdom?
    a) Dwarka
    b) Taxila
    c) Kurukshetra
    d) Ayodhya

13. Whose devotee was Prahlada?
    a) Vishnu

b) Brahma
c) Shiva
d) Indra

14. Who once wore a garland of consonants and vowels?
a) Lakshmi
b) Saraswati
c) Kali
d) Draupadi

15. Who assists Yama by keeping records of deeds of people?
a) Chitragupta
b) Indra
c) Ganesha
d) Brahma

16. In the Ramayana, venu, mridang, dundubhi and shankha were names of ...
a) Sita's sisters
b) Musical instruments
c) Chapters
d) Arjuna's bows

17. Which god is the creator of the universe?
a) Shiva
b) Indra
c) Vishnu
d) Brahma

18. Dhananjaya was another name of ...
a) Bhima

b) Arjuna
c) Nakula
d) Sahadeva

19. Who was the seventh incarnation of Mahavishnu?
a) Krishna
b) Rama
c) Vamana
d) Narasimha

20. Which Hindu deity is also known as Gangadhara, Chandrasekhara and Trilochana?
a) Vishnu
b) Shiva
c) Krishna
d) Brahma

HUMAN BODY

1. In which organ of the human body would you find the aqueous humour?
a) Eyes
b) Liver
c) Kidneys
d) Heart

2. A geriatrician deals with the health and care of ...
a) Babies
b) Teenagers
c) New mothers
d) Old people

3. More than half of the bones in the human body are found in your ...
a) Hands and feet
b) Ribs

c) Face
d) Ears

4. The jejunum and the ileum are parts of what in the human body?
   a) Stomach
   b) Liver
   c) Small intestine
   d) Large intestine

5. In which part of the body are the two sensory organs of balance located?
   a) Heart
   b) Ears
   c) Eyes
   d) Nose

6. The colour of our eyes depends on the amount of melanin in the...
   a) Retina
   b) Iris
   c) Cornea
   d) Toenail

7. Which of these tools shares its name with a small bone in the ears?
   a) Hammer
   b) Pliers
   c) Knife
   d) Handsaw

8. In the human body, the longest and strongest bones are found in the ...
   a) Legs
   b) Heart
   c) Arms
   d) Head

9. How many ribs does a human being have?
   a) Twenty-four
   b) Thirty
   c) Forty-one
   d) Forty-five

10. The primary function of the hyoid bone in the human body is to support the ...
   a) Appendix
   b) Thigh
   c) Big toe
   d) Tongue

11. Which part of the human body has the thinnest skin?
   a) Lips
   b) Eyelids
   c) Palms
   d) Nose

12. Which of these parts of the human body is about 22–25 feet in length?
   a) Large intestine
   b) Stomach

c) Small intestine
d) Liver

13. In the human body, which organ's primary function is to remove waste and excess water?
a) Heart
b) Liver
c) Large intestine
d) Kidneys

14. Which of these is a projection at the front of the neck?
a) Adam's apple
b) Islets of Langerhans
c) Bowman's capsule
d) Achilles tendon

15. Which is the most commonly tested part of the body?
a) Heart
b) Blood
c) Liver
d) Eyes

16. In the human body, the size of what increases during mental activities in proportion to the difficulty of a task?
a) Fingernails
b) Pupils
c) Hair
d) Teeth

17. In the human body, ball, socket and hinge are types of . . .
a) Fats

b) Muscles
c) Joints
d) Cells

18. In which part of the human body would you find calf muscles?
a) Cheeks
b) Legs
c) Abdomen
d) Fingers

19. Which vitamin is required by the human body to form clots and to stop bleeding?
a) Vitamin A
b) Vitamin B
c) Vitamin C
d) Vitamin K

20. Which of these shares its name with a bone in the human body?
a) Diameter
b) Radius
c) Hypotenuse
d) Perimeter

INDIA

1. Which of these languages is not represented on the language panel of Indian banknotes?
   a) Bhojpuri
   b) Urdu
   c) Bengali
   d) Tamil

2. Which of these states of India has only two districts?
   a) West Bengal
   b) Sikkim
   c) Goa
   d) Uttar Pradesh

3. Before the Supreme Court of India moved to its present building, where did it function from?
   a) Parliament House

b) Rashtrapati Bhavan
c) Red Fort
d) Charminar

4. In which state is the Rajaji National Park located?
   a) Assam
   b) Uttarakhand
   c) Madhya Pradesh
   d) Karnataka

5. In which language was the national anthem of India originally written?
   a) Hindi
   b) English
   c) Tamil
   d) Bengali

6. Ib in Odisha and Od in Gujarat are the ...
   a) Shortest names of railway stations
   b) Smallest towns in India
   c) Largest towns in India
   d) Largest ports in India

7. Which of these songs was a part of Bankim Chandra Chatterji's famous novel *Anandamath*?
   a) 'Vande Mataram'
   b) 'Kadam Kadam Badhaye Ja'
   c) 'Hum Honge Kamyaab'
   d) 'Jana Gana Mana'

8. Which word comes from the Sanskrit words meaning 'bowing action'?
a) Swagatam
b) Shukriya
c) Alvida
d) Namaskar

9. Which post in India have G.V. Mavalankar, N. Sanjiva Reddy and P.A. Sangma all held?
a) Chairman of the Rajya Sabha
b) Chief Justice of India
c) Speaker, Lok Sabha
d) Governor, RBI

10. Who was the first chief of staff of the Indian Army after India became independent?
a) Sukumar Sen
b) K.M. Cariappa
c) H.J. Kania
d) Satish Dhawan

11. What did the Royal Bengal tiger replace as the national animal of India?
a) Indian rhinoceros
b) Elephant
c) Asiatic lion
d) Indian spotted deer

12. How many digits are there in the Aadhaar number issued by UIDAI?
a) Twelve

b) Fourteen
c) Sixteen
d) Eighteen

13. Which of these should be made of handspun and handwoven khadi by law in India?
a) Currency note
b) National flag
c) Nehru jacket
d) Gandhi cap

14. According to the Indian national calendar, the first day of a year in a non-leap year coincides with . . .
a) 1 January
b) 22 March
c) 15 April
d) 29 February

15. Which organization traces its origin to the Special Police Establishment that was set up in 1941?
a) CBI
b) RBI
c) NCC
d) BSF

16. In the Indian Navy, what are Rajput, Rana, Ranvir, Ranjit and Ranvijay as a group?
a) Horses
b) Ships
c) Fighter jets
d) Salutes

17. Which is the only state in India that is larger than Madhya Pradesh in terms of area?
a) Tamil Nadu
b) Uttar Pradesh
c) Rajasthan
d) Manipur

18. Which of these cities is so named because Laxman is said to have cut off Surpanakha's nose there?
a) Almora
b) Nainital
c) Nashik
d) Patna

19. According to the 2011 census, which is the least populous state in India?
a) Goa
b) Manipur
c) Tamil Nadu
d) Sikkim

20. On which river in Assam is Majuli, a freshwater river island, located?
a) The Ganges
b) Krishna
c) Brahmaputra
d) Kaveri

INDIAN HISTORY I

1. Which event started on 12 March 1930 and lasted for twenty-four days?
   a) The first Asian Games
   b) Census of India
   c) The Khilafat Movement
   d) Dandi March

2. Which historical place is a small village in the Navsari district of Gujarat?
   a) Chauri Chaura
   b) Malgudi
   c) Dandi
   d) Noakhali

3. What measured 1500 km in length from Sonar Gaon in Bengal to the Indus River in the west?
   a) The Ganges

b) Deccan Plateau
c) The Grand Trunk Road
d) Great Wall of China

4. According to legend, Ramachandra Pandurang's name was changed when Bajirao II gave him a ...
   a) Cap
   b) Cannon
   c) Sword
   d) Horse

5. The name of which historical movement in India literally means 'land gift'?
   a) Appiko
   b) Bhoodan
   c) Chipko
   d) Navdanya

6. Whose tomb lies at a distance of two kilometres west of Haldighati?
   a) Chetak
   b) Bucephalus
   c) Humayun
   d) Shivaji

7. What name did Subhas Chandra Bose give to the Andaman and Nicobar Islands?
   a) Swaraj and Shaheed Islands
   b) Surya and Chandra Islands
   c) Yash and Gaurav Islands
   d) Jeet and Amar Islands

8. In which city was the Japanese advance into India halted in 1944?
a) Kohima
b) Kolkata
c) Guwahati
d) Patna

9. Which popular queen was the wife of Raja Gangadhar Rao?
a) Jodha Bai
b) Ahilyabai Holkar
c) Rani Padmini
d) Rani Lakshmibai

10. Who made a momentous decision to adopt the attire of a poor peasant in Madurai on 22 September 1921?
a) Vallabhbhai Patel
b) Jawaharlal Nehru
c) Mahatma Gandhi
d) King George VI

11. Which present-day hill station was formerly part of the kingdom of Sikkim?
a) Ooty
b) Darjeeling
c) Nainital
d) Shimla

12. In 1864, which city did John Lawrence make the summer capital of British India?
a) Srinagar
b) Shimla

c) Kolkata
d) Mumbai

13. The fifth Sikh guru, Arjan Dev, laid the foundation of which of these landmarks?
    a) Lotus Temple
    b) Golden Temple
    c) Meenakshi Temple
    d) Sun Temple

14. What kind of a tree is the Bo tree or the Bodhi tree?
    a) Coconut
    b) Mango
    c) Pipal
    d) Neem

15. The Humayun Gate and the Talaqi Gate are gateways to which monument?
    a) Purana Qila
    b) Jama Masjid
    c) Red Fort
    d) Taj Mahal

16. Which present-day city is the site of the historical cities Tughlakabad and Shahjahanabad?
    a) Patna
    b) Kolkata
    c) New Delhi
    d) Cuttack

17. The Lion Capital of Sarnath is a specimen of the art of which dynasty?
a) Gupta
b) Maurya
c) Maya
d) Kushan

18. In 1893, who delivered a famous speech at the World's Parliament of Religions in Chicago?
a) Sri Chaitanya
b) Sant Kabir
c) Guru Ram Das
d) Swami Vivekananda

19. Which of these battles was fought between the Marathas and the Afghans?
a) First Battle of Panipat
b) Battle of Plassey
c) Third Battle of Panipat
d) Battle of Haldighati

20. Whose first sermon is called 'Dharmachakra Pravartana Sutra'?
a) Mahavira
b) Buddha
c) Guru Nanak
d) Shankaracharya

INDIAN HISTORY II

1. In Dandi, on the shore of which waterbody did Mahatma Gandhi break the salt law?
   a) The Bay of Bengal
   b) The Ganges
   c) Narmada
   d) The Arabian Sea

2. Which city served as the capital of the United Provinces of British India between 1904 and 1949?
   a) Varanasi
   b) Prayagraj
   c) Kanpur
   d) Agra

3. By what name is Narendranath Dutta better known?
   a) Osho
   b) Mahesh Yogi

c) Swami Vivekananda
d) Vidyasagar

4. *The Feather of the Dawn* is a collection of English poems by . . .
a) Mahadevi Varma
b) Sarojini Naidu
c) Indira Gandhi
d) Amrita Pritam

5. Who among these was also known by the name Vishnugupta?
a) Ashoka
b) Kautilya
c) Kalidasa
d) Samudragupta

6. Which among these was the capital of the Pandyas?
a) Warangal
b) Vatapi
c) Pataliputra
d) Madurai

7. Who killed Afzal Khan, a general of the sultan of Bijapur, with 'tiger claws'?
a) Iltutmish
b) Tipu Sultan
c) Sher Shah Suri
d) Shivaji

8. Which religion is Theravada a form of?
a) Buddhism

b) Baha'i
c) Jainism
d) Taoism

9. What was the name of Gautam Buddha's wife?
   a) Ruma
   b) Yashodhara
   c) Urmila
   d) Ahalya

10. Which monument, located near Quwwat-ul Islam Mosque, has 379 steps?
    a) Red Fort
    b) Agra Fort
    c) Qutub Minar
    d) Taj Mahal

11. The Group of Monuments at Mahabalipuram was built during the rule of the ...
    a) Chalukyas
    b) Cholas
    c) Pallavas
    d) Guptas

12. In which state is Champaran, the site of the indigo rebellion?
    a) Bihar
    b) Madhya Pradesh
    c) Assam
    d) Tripura

13. Amoghavarsha I, the author of a part of the *Kavirajamarga*, was a ruler of which dynasty?
a) Chola
b) Chalukya
c) Rashtrakuta
d) Yadava

14. For whom was the Peacock Throne built?
a) Jahangir
b) Shah Jahan
c) Akbar
d) Humayun

15. Which state was formed in 1956 with the merger of the erstwhile Travancore–Cochin state and the Malabar district?
a) Kerala
b) Karnataka
c) Tamil Nadu
d) Maharashtra

16. In which of these places were two important battles fought by the Mughals?
a) Varanasi
b) Kalinga
c) Panipat
d) Patna

17. In 1602, what was erected to commemorate Akbar's conquest over Deccan?
a) Qutub Minar
b) Buland Darwaza

c) Charminar
d) Gol Gumbaz

18. Which governor general waged the Fourth Anglo–Mysore War?
a) Warren Hastings
b) William Bentick
c) Charles Cornwallis
d) Richard Wellesley

19. Which foreign power conquered Diu in 1546 and ruled there till 1961?
a) German
b) Portuguese
c) Dutch
d) French

20. Who wrote the epic poem *Prithviraj Raso*?
a) Chand Bardai
b) Vidyapati
c) Kabir
d) Surdas

LANGUAGE

1. In which language did R.K. Narayan write most of his works?
   a) Hindi
   b) English
   c) Kannada
   d) Punjabi

2. In the language of the apes, whose name means 'white skin'?
   a) Mowgli
   b) Peter Pan
   c) Tarzan
   d) Goldilocks

3. The name of which part of a building comes from a Latin word meaning 'to run'?
   a) Corridor
   b) Veranda

c) Window
d) Lobby

4. Which emoji was adjudged the Oxford Dictionaries' Word of the Year in 2015?
a) Winking
b) Tears of joy
c) Smiling with sunglasses
d) Thinking face

5. Seals, walruses and sea lions belong to the order called Pinnipedia. What does Pinnipedia mean?
a) Long-tooth
b) Soft-skin
c) Wing-foot
d) Hairy-one

6. Which language is also known in some areas as 'Gorkha Bhasa'?
a) Konkani
b) Nepali
c) Manipuri
d) Maithili

7. Which term comes from a medieval Latin word meaning 'manual or book of words'?
a) Calendar
b) Dictionary
c) Atlas
d) Directory

8. In English, which of these punctuation marks is represented by two dots?
   a) Semicolon
   b) Comma
   c) Exclamation mark
   d) Colon

9. What do you call a word or phrase that is made by arranging the letters of another word or phrase in a different order?
   a) Oxymoron
   b) Simile
   c) Anagram
   d) Metaphor

10. Which of these words comes from a Latin word meaning 'more'?
   a) Plus
   b) Minus
   c) Cos
   d) Pi

11. Which is the official and most widely spoken language of Mexico?
   a) Italian
   b) Portuguese
   c) Spanish
   d) German

12. Which author is credited with popularizing expressions like 'foregone conclusion' and 'wild goose chase'?
   a) Lewis Carroll

b) Thomas Hardy
c) Charles Dickens
d) William Shakespeare

13. The name of which of these places means 'land of the thunderbolt' in Tibetan?
a) Nainital
b) Ooty
c) Darjeeling
d) Mount Abu

14. Which of these words is associated with the region immediately beneath the skin?
a) Hypodermic
b) Haemophilia
c) Dementia
d) Vaccination

15. Which word can be used to describe a book of maps and the topmost vertebra of the human backbone?
a) Topograph
b) Atlas
c) Globe
d) Axis

16. Which term gets its name from a Greek word meaning 'number'?
a) Astronomy
b) Arithmetic
c) Mensuration
d) Algebra

17. Which is the third most spoken language in the world?
a) French
b) Hindi
c) Spanish
d) Bengali

18. In an alphabetical list of state capitals in India, the name of which state capital would come last?
a) Maharashtra
b) West Bengal
c) Tamil Nadu
d) Kerala

19. Which word can be used to describe a punctuation mark, the large intestine and the currency of Costa Rica?
a) Asterisk
b) Colon
c) Apostrophe
d) Full stop

20. Which of these words can be used to describe a British admiral, a wrestling hold and a port in New Zealand?
a) Clive
b) Nelson
c) Washington
d) Lincoln

LEADERS

1. Whose autobiography is titled *Toward Freedom*?
   a) Jawaharlal Nehru
   b) Subhas Chandra Bose
   c) Annie Besant
   d) Vallabhbhai Patel

2. If Margaret Thatcher was the first woman prime minister of the United Kingdom, who was the second?
   a) Angela Merkel
   b) Nancy Astor
   c) Theresa May
   d) Camilla Parker

3. In 1899, who was sent to cover the Boer War in South Africa by London's The *Morning Post*?
   a) Winston Churchill
   b) Vladimir Lenin

c) Mikhail Gorbachev
d) Nelson Mandela

4. Which US president did not live in the White House?
a) George Washington
b) Abraham Lincoln
c) Thomas Jefferson
d) James Monroe

5. Who did Manmohan Singh refer to as the 'Bhishma Pitamah of Indian politics'?
a) Mahatma Gandhi
b) Atal Bihari Vajpayee
c) Rahul Gandhi
d) Himself

6. Who went to Natal in 1893 to serve a merchant named Dada Abdulla?
a) Jawaharlal Nehru
b) Mahatma Gandhi
c) Vallabhbhai Patel
d) Dhirubhai Ambani

7. Which was the first foreign country to issue postage stamps with Gandhiji's picture?
a) South Africa
b) United States
c) United Kingdom
d) France

8. Whose autobiography is titled *India Wins Freedom*?
   a) Vallabhbhai Patel
   b) Abul Kalam Azad
   c) Bal Gangadhar Tilak
   d) Lala Lajpat Rai

9. Which famous person once said: 'By blood, I am Albanian. By citizenship, an Indian. As to my calling, I belong to the world'?
   a) Nelson Mandela
   b) Jawaharlal Nehru
   c) Mother Teresa
   d) Mahatma Gandhi

10. Who wrote the book *Painting as a Pastime*?
   a) Adolf Hitler
   b) Albert Einstein
   c) Winston Churchill
   d) Mahatma Gandhi

11. Which of these countries had rulers primarily addressed by the title of Czar?
   a) Spain
   b) Germany
   c) Japan
   d) Russia

12. Which American president gave the White House its official name?
   a) Franklin Roosevelt
   b) Abraham Lincoln

c) Gerald Ford
d) Theodore Roosevelt

13. Which leader's father was a senior economist for the government of Kenya?
a) Angela Merkel
b) Sheikh Hasina
c) Barack Obama
d) Aung San Suu Kyi

14. Where is Sheikh Mujibur Rahman regarded as the 'father of the nation'?
a) Pakistan
b) Bangladesh
c) Bahrain
d) Kuwait

15. How do we better know Tenzin Gyatso?
a) Sunil Chhetri
b) Bhaichung Bhutia
c) Barack Obama
d) Dalai Lama

16. Nelson Mandela said, '_____ is the most powerful weapon which you can use to change the world.' Fill in the blank.
a) Imagination
b) Perseverance
c) Education
d) Action

17. Gandhiji wrote that we must learn to live and die like Socrates, and referred to him as a great . . .
a) Swadeshi
b) Sangrami
c) Satyagrahi
d) Sadhu

18. Whom did Mahatma Gandhi refer to as 'the one person in the world who can prevent a war'?
a) Himself
b) Napoleon
c) The Pope
d) Adolf Hitler

19. Which country's monarch is known as the Druk Gyalpo or Dragon King?
a) Sri Lanka
b) Bhutan
c) Nepal
d) Myanmar

20. Who voted for the first time in his/her life on 27 April 1994, at the age of seventy-five?
a) Dalai Lama
b) Nelson Mandela
c) Mother Teresa
d) Bill Clinton

LITERATURE

1. In the novel *Animal Farm*, what kind of an animal is Napoleon?
   a) Pig
   b) Sheep
   c) Horse
   d) Kangaroo

2. Which present-day city was Rudyard Kipling born in?
   a) Mumbai
   b) Kolkata
   c) Hyderabad
   d) New Delhi

3. Which of these is not the title of an autobiography?
   a) *Wings of Fire*
   b) *Long Walk to Freedom*

c) *The Diary of a Young Girl*
d) *A Brief History of Time*

4. The name of which legendary prince of Denmark, a hero in a Shakespearean play, also means a small village?
   a) Romeo
   b) Hamlet
   c) Macbeth
   d) Henry

5. In which novel would you meet characters named Jim Hawkins and Billy Bones?
   a) *Oliver Twist*
   b) *Treasure Island*
   c) *Robinson Crusoe*
   d) *Ivanhoe*

6. Who was made a prisoner on the island of Lilliput?
   a) Alice
   b) Swami
   c) Gulliver
   d) Robin Hood

7. Who got the idea for *The Hunger Games* as she was channel-hopping at home?
   a) J.K. Rowling
   b) Suzanne Collins
   c) C.S. Lewis
   d) Zadie Smith

8. About which famous author did Leo Tolstoy write: 'I remember the astonishment I felt when I first read _____ ... not only did I feel no delight, but I felt an irresistible repulsion and tedium...'? Fill in the blank.
a) Karl Marx
b) William Shakespeare
c) Rudyard Kipling
d) Charles Dickens

9. Which famous novel begins with the line: 'It was the best of times, it was the worst of times...'?
a) *War and Peace*
b) *Alice's Adventures in Wonderland*
c) *The Adventures of Huckleberry Finn*
d) *A Tale of Two Cities*

10. Who received the Sahitya Akademi Award for his book *The Shadow Lines*?
a) Amitav Ghosh
b) Arundhati Roy
c) Devdutt Pattanaik
d) Chetan Bhagat

11. *Mitrabheda*, *Mitralabha* and *Kakolukiyam* are divisions of which of these books?
a) Arthashastra
b) Panchatantra
c) Natyashastra
d) The Jataka Tales

12. In the Harry Potter films, which character has been played by Ralph Fiennes, Christian Coulson and Richard Bremmer?
a) Lord Voldemort
b) Vernon Dursley
c) Albus Dumbledore
d) Nicolas Flamel

13. Of all these characters created by William Shakespeare, who has the most lines to deliver?
a) Lady Macbeth
b) Hamlet
c) Othello
d) Romeo

14. Which literary character eats a cake marked 'Eat Me,' which causes her to grow really tall?
a) Alice
b) Thumbelina
c) Rapunzel
d) Cheshire Cat

15. What kind of place is Azkaban in the Harry Potter series?
a) A prison
b) A bank
c) A school
d) A wand shop

16. Which book was translated as *Kalila wa-Dimna* in Arabic?
a) *Pride and Prejudice*
b) Panchatantra

c) *Gita Govinda*

d) Arthashastra

17. In one of Shakespeare's works, whose name is used to describe a moneylender charging high rates of interest?

a) Hamlet

b) Shylock

c) Romeo

d) Lady Macbeth

18. *The Bachelor of Arts* was R.K. Narayan's second novel. Which was his first book?

a) *Malgudi Days*

b) *The Man-Eater of Malgudi*

c) *The Guide*

d) *Swami and Friends*

19. Which work by Shakespeare is considered unlucky as it is believed that the lines contain magic spells?

a) *Macbeth*

b) *Hamlet*

c) *The Merchant of Venice*

d) *David Copperfield*

20. 'Road Song of the Bandar-Log' and 'Hunting-Song of the Seeonee Pack' are chapters of . . .

a) *Tarzan of the Apes*

b) *Moby Dick*

c) *Black Beauty*

d) *The Jungle Book*

MIXED BAG I

1. Who received the Bharat Ratna in 1990, the Nobel Peace Prize in 1993 and the Gandhi Peace Prize in 2000?
   a) Dalai Lama
   b) Nelson Mandela
   c) Mother Teresa
   d) Aung San Suu Kyi

2. In 1920, the League of Nations internationally standardized the format of ...
   a) Driving licences
   b) Shoes
   c) Traffic signals
   d) Passports

3. What was known by names such as gola and satha in the eighteenth century?
   a) Onion

b) Potato
c) Cauliflower
d) Radish

4. According to the NATO phonetic alphabet, what is the code word for the letter 'I'?
a) Indonesia
b) Iran
c) India
d) Islamabad

5. Which of these is generally eaten with makke di roti?
a) Bhatura
b) Pizza
c) Biryani
d) Sarson da saag

6. After China and India, which is the third most populous country in the world?
a) Brazil
b) United States
c) Russia
d) Vatican City

7. Which country's national anthem did Abu-Al-Asar Hafeez Jalandhari write?
a) Bangladesh
b) Nepal
c) Indonesia
d) Pakistan

8. The value and durability of the Kashmiri carpet depends on the ...
   a) Amount of thread used
   b) Knots per square inch
   c) Number of colours used
   d) Amount of snowfall

9. In Venice, a gondola is a type of ...
   a) Boat
   b) Stringed instrument
   c) Sweet
   d) Paper

10. What are bond, bristol and kraft varieties of?
   a) Combs
   b) Handkerchiefs
   c) Paper
   d) Shoes

11. Written in AD 800, what did Lu Yu's first book centre around?
   a) Silk
   b) Tea
   c) Kangaroos
   d) Quizzing

12. In most cars, which of these is controlled by the driver's foot?
   a) Indicator lights
   b) Wiper
   c) Clutch
   d) Gear

13. Who among these developed a system of writing for the blind?
a) Louis Braille
b) Helen Keller
c) Alexander Graham Bell
d) James Cook

14. In 2003, who received honorary Nepali citizenship in recognition of his services to the people of the Solukhumbu region?
a) Edmund Hillary
b) Mother Teresa
c) Neil Armstrong
d) Abraham Lincoln

15. Accidentally invented by Thomas Sullivan, which of these has 2000 perforations or small holes?
a) Mosquito nets
b) Teabags
c) Postage stamps
d) Beehives

16. Which country's national anthem is 'Sayaun Thunga Phool Ka'?
a) Bhutan
b) Nepal
c) Sri Lanka
d) Maldives

17. Which colour appears between blue and yellow in a rainbow?
a) Red
b) Green

c) Orange
d) Indigo

18. In India, which profession would you pursue with an LLB degree?
a) Medicine
b) Law
c) Architecture
d) Quizzing

19. What comes in two basic shapes: snowflake and mushroom?
a) Pasta
b) Cake
c) Ice cream
d) Popped popcorn

20. If a Britisher calls it an aubergine and Americans call it an eggplant, what do we usually call it?
a) Cauliflower
b) Potato
c) Brinjal
d) Cabbage

MIXED BAG II

1. Which country has changed its national flag the most number of times in the twentieth century?
a) Afghanistan
b) Sri Lanka
c) Nepal
d) United States

2. Which colour is common to the flags of Bangladesh, Switzerland and Japan?
a) Green
b) Red
c) Orange
d) White

3. Which of these birds gets its pink colour from the shrimplike crustaceans that it eats?
a) Ostrich

b) Crow
c) Flamingo
d) Hummingbird

4. In which organ is bile, a greenish-yellow secretion, produced?
a) Liver
b) Lungs
c) Heart
d) Pancreas

5. The four flags planted by Tenzing Norgay and Edmund Hillary on Mount Everest were those of the UK, Nepal, India and the . . .
a) United Nations
b) Red Cross
c) World Health Organization
d) European Union

6. Which city connects the Kumbh Mela and Anand Bhavan, the home of the Nehrus?
a) Nashik
b) Prayagraj
c) Ujjain
d) Mumbai

7. Which is the most commonly transplanted organ in the human body?
a) Liver
b) Ears
c) Kidneys
d) Lungs

8. The wings of which of these birds have modified into flippers?
   a) Ostriches
   b) Penguins
   c) Hens
   d) Pelicans

9. Which structure in the human body is surrounded by periodontal tissues?
   a) Heart
   b) Teeth
   c) Lungs
   d) Liver

10. In which state of India would you find districts named Korea and Bastar?
   a) Chhattisgarh
   b) Jharkhand
   c) Madhya Pradesh
   d) Kerala

11. Traditionally, which of these sweets is soaked in milk?
   a) Jalebi
   b) Rasgulla
   c) Lollipop
   d) Rasmalai

12. Which part of the human body secretes hydrochloric acid to kill the bacteria in food?
   a) Liver
   b) Stomach

c) Small intestine
d) Pancreas

13. Medulla oblongata is the lowest part of the ...
a) Brain
b) Kidneys
c) Liver
d) Nose

14. Which is the first Indian state to see the sun rise?
a) Mizoram
b) Arunachal Pradesh
c) West Bengal
d) Maharashtra

15. The islets of Langerhans are embedded in the ...
a) Pancreas
b) Kidneys
c) Liver
d) Spleen

16. Which of these is sometimes called Vilaayati Baingan?
a) Tomato
b) Onion
c) Ladies' fingers
d) Bitter gourd

17. Which is the only country in the modern world that does not have a rectangular national flag?
a) Cambodia
b) United Kingdom

c) New Zealand
d) Nepal

18. Which part of the human body contains about one hundred million photoreceptors?
a) Tongue
b) Nose
c) Eyes
d) Ears

19. In India, Kanthari, Kashmiri, Jwala and Dhani varieties of which spice?
a) Chilli
b) Vanilla
c) Cardamom
d) Ginger

20. Which country is known for the Cantonese and Schezwan cooking styles?
a) Japan
b) China
c) Italy
d) Portugal

MUSIC

1. Who among these was part of a rhythm band named Planet Drum along with Mickey Hart, Sikiru Adepoju and Giovanni Hidalgo?
   a) Bismillah Khan
   b) Pannalal Ghosh
   c) Hariprasad Chaurasia
   d) Zakir Hussain

2. Which famous musician is believed to have invented the tabla?
   a) Tansen
   b) Mirza Ghalib
   c) Amir Khusrau
   d) Faiz Ahmed Faiz

3. On hearing about whose death did Ravi Shankar compose 'Farewell My Friend'?
   a) Mahatma Gandhi
   b) Lady Diana
   c) Satyajit Ray
   d) John F. Kennedy

4. Who, after winning a Grammy, said, 'I've been appreciated only twice by my guru, my father, the late Ustad Allah Rakha'?
   a) Bismillah Khan
   b) Shiv Kumar Sharma
   c) Allauddin Khan
   d) Zakir Hussain

5. Which musical instrument is known as *klavier* in German?
   a) Piano
   b) Trumpet
   c) Mouth organ
   d) Guitar

6. Which musician of India forms the basis of the book *Abba . . . God's Greatest Gift to Us*?
   a) Bismillah Khan
   b) Amjad Ali Khan
   c) Rashid Khan
   d) Zakir Hussain

7. In Indian classical music, which note comes just before 'Re'?
   a) Pa
   b) Ga

c) So
d) Sa

8. Which of these is a stringed instrument?
   a) Tabla
   b) Ektara
   c) Mridangam
   d) Duffli

9. What are Bhairavi, Asavari and Todi types of?
   a) Martial art forms
   b) Rivers
   c) Sarods
   d) Classical ragas

10. Which of these instruments is generally held with one hand and played with the other?
    a) Tabla
    b) Xylophone
    c) Mridangam
    d) Duffli

11. Which of these is a wind instrument?
    a) Violin
    b) Mandolin
    c) Sitar
    d) Bansuri

12. Who was the music director of All India Radio, New Delhi from 1949 to 1956?
    a) Ravi Shankar

b) Bismillah Khan
c) Shiv Kumar Sharma
d) Zakir Hussain

13. According to legend, the ravanastram, a stringed instrument made by Ravana, inspired which modern-day instrument?
a) Violin
b) Sitar
c) Santoor
d) Bagpipes

14. In 2002, who published his autobiography titled *Journey with a Hundred Strings: My Life in Music*?
a) Ravi Shankar
b) Allah Rakha
c) Amjad Ali Khan
d) Shiv Kumar Sharma

15. Which of these is a percussion instrument?
a) Sarod
b) Mridangam
c) Sarangi
d) Shehnai

16. Who sang as a playback singer in the 1956 film *Basant Bahar*?
a) Ravi Shankar
b) M.S. Subbulakshmi
c) Bhimsen Joshi
d) Zakir Hussain

17. The book *Bapi ... The Love of My Life* is a daughter's tribute to ...
a) Amjad Ali Khan
b) Bismillah Khan
c) Ravi Shankar
d) Hariprasad Chaurasia

18. Which of these is a conical double-reed aerophone of southern India?
a) Nagaswaram
b) Tabla
c) Harmonium
d) Sarangi

19. According to legend, what was created when the pakhawaj accidentally split into two parts?
a) The ghatam
b) The dholak
c) The tabla
d) The nagara

20. In whose honour did Ravi Shankar create the raga Mohan Kauns?
a) Dhyan Chand
b) Lord Krishna
c) Himself
d) Mahatma Gandhi

MYTHOLOGY

1. Who did Thetis dip into the Styx to render him invulnerable?
   a) Achilles
   b) Thor
   c) Osiris
   d) Bellerophon

2. In Greek mythology, who is the goddess of reason, wisdom and war?
   a) Athena
   b) Artemis
   c) Hera
   d) Demeter

3. In ancient Greek mythology, what is the traditional weapon of Zeus?
   a) Sword
   b) Thunderbolt

c) Hammer
d) Trident

4. In Greek mythology, who is the god of the sea?
   a) Hades
   b) Ares
   c) Dionysus
   d) Poseidon

5. One of the Seven Wonders of the Ancient World, the Statue of Zeus, was located in . . .
   a) Greece
   b) Italy
   c) Germany
   d) France

6. Which of these planets is named after the Roman goddess of love and beauty?
   a) Mars
   b) Uranus
   c) Venus
   d) Earth

7. In Roman mythology, who is the god of commerce, travel and thievery?
   a) Earth
   b) Venus
   c) Mercury
   d) Saturn

8. Which planet is blue in colour and is named after the Roman god of the sea?

a) Neptune

b) Uranus

c) Saturn

d) Jupiter

9. In Greek mythology, chimera had the head of which animal?

a) Tiger

b) Lion

c) Snake

d) Fox

10. Name the winged horse that sprang from the blood of the gorgon Medusa as she was beheaded by the hero Perseus.

a) Cupid

b) Pegasus

c) Phoenix

d) Harpy

11. Who killed the monster Minotaur?

a) Bellerophon

b) Theseus

c) Odysseus

d) Heracles

12. Killing which nine-headed serpent was one of the twelve tasks of Heracles?

a) Triton

b) Hydra

c) Charon

d) Sphinx

13. Which of these creature's face turned anyone that looked at it into stone?

a) Scylla

b) Medusa

c) Charybdis

d) Cerberus

14. In Greek mythology, who was the first woman?

a) Pandora

b) Aphrodite

c) Isis

d) Athena

15. In Norse mythology, what is the hall of slain warriors called?

a) El Dorado

b) Valhalla

c) Atlantis

d) Nysa

16. In English, which day of the week is named after the wife of Odin and mother of Balder?

a) Wednesday

b) Thursday

c) Friday

d) Saturday

17. According to Plutarch, Osiris was slain or drowned by . . .

a) Horus

b) Apollo
c) Prometheus
d) Seth

18. The Colossus of Rhodes was the statue of Helios . . .
a) The sun god
b) The god of warfare
c) The god of agriculture
d) The god of the underworld

19. In Greek religion, whose name meant Forethinker?
a) Adam
b) Prometheus
c) Achilles
d) Helios

20. With which city did King Priam of Troy's son share his name?
a) Paris
b) Rome
c) Berlin
d) London

NATURE

1. According to legend, the absence of which insect gave Silent Valley National Park in Kerala its name?
   a) Mosquito
   b) Firefly
   c) Cicada
   d) Honeybee

2. In 1830, the northern boundary of which forest in Asia came to be known as the Dampier-Hodges Line?
   a) Sundarbans
   b) Kaziranga
   c) Nottingham
   d) Gir

3. The spectacular aurora borealis is also called the ...
   a) Southern Lights
   b) Northern Lights

c) Western Lights
d) Eastern Lights

4. Its natural habitat is only in a small part of China and the Chinese name for this animal translates to 'large bear cat'. Which one of the following is it?
a) Porcupine
b) Raccoon
c) Giant panda
d) Koala

5. Which is the oldest national park in India?
a) Yellowstone National Park
b) Gir National Park
c) Kaziranga National Park
d) Jim Corbett National Park

6. The state Kerala is said to have been named after which tree?
a) Mango
b) Date
c) Coconut
d) Neem

7. Also known as Ayers Rock, which landmark is famous for appearing to change colour at different times of the day and year?
a) Uluru
b) Stonehenge
c) The Rock Garden of Chandigarh
d) Victoria Falls

8. Which fibre is produced from the plants of the genus *Gossypium*?
   a) Mohair
   b) Jute
   c) Cotton
   d) Wool

9. Which waterfall was called Mosi-oa-Tunya or 'The Smoke That Thunders' by the local people?
   a) Victoria Falls
   b) Angel Falls
   c) Jog Falls
   d) Niagara Falls

10. Which of these products is obtained from plants?
   a) Honey
   b) Silk
   c) Rubber
   d) Lac

11. The well-known Kaziranga National Park harbours the world's largest population of which animal?
   a) Asiatic lion
   b) Indian rhinoceros
   c) Nilgai
   d) Gharial

12. A leaf of which tree appears on the flag of Canada?
   a) Teak
   b) Sal

c) Pine

d) Maple

13. Which of these takes the most time to break apart?
   a) Paper napkin
   b) Tin can
   c) Glass bottle
   d) Nylon fabric

14. The Great Barrier Reef, which contains the world's largest collection of coral reefs, is in ...
   a) United States
   b) Australia
   c) Brazil
   d) Spain

15. Which of these national parks is located in India?
   a) Jim Corbett National Park
   b) Sagarmatha National Park
   c) Yellowstone National Park
   d) Serengeti National Park

16. Which of the following make up a quarter of all mammals?
   a) Bats
   b) Bears
   c) Elephants
   d) Orangutans

17. Which canyon, cut by the Colorado River, is noted for its fantastic shapes and colouration?
   a) Grand Canyon

b) The Great Barrier Reef
c) Paricutin
d) Stonehenge

18. The Spanish explorers gave which edible plant product a name meaning 'grinning face'?
a) Coconut
b) Watermelon
c) Papaya
d) Guava

19. According to the Guinness World Records, which was the most forested country in the world in 2005 in terms of actual land area covered by forest?
a) Bhutan
b) Brazil
c) Congo
d) China

20. Where would you come across landmarks called Yellow Band and Geneva Spur?
a) Mount Everest
b) Sahara Desert
c) The moon
d) Antarctica

NOBEL PRIZE

1. Which Nobel laureate started an experimental school at Shantiniketan, West Bengal?
   a) Amartya Sen
   b) Rabindranath Tagore
   c) C.V. Raman
   d) Mother Teresa

2. Who among these Nobel laureates was not born in India?
   a) Ronald Ross
   b) Rudyard Kipling
   c) Mother Teresa
   d) Amartya Sen

3. Which yesteryear Indian politician was nominated for the Nobel Prize in Literature from 1933 to 1937?
   a) Jawaharlal Nehru
   b) C. Rajagopalachari

c) S. Radhakrishnan

d) Atal Bihari Vajpayee

4. Till 2020, how many US Presidents were awarded the Nobel Peace Prize?
   a) Two
   b) Three
   c) Four
   d) Five

5. Which Nobel Prize has never been shared by three laureates?
   a) Peace
   b) Literature
   c) Economic Sciences
   d) Chemistry

6. On whose death anniversary is International Day of Charity observed?
   a) Marie Curie
   b) Mother Teresa
   c) Henry Dunant
   d) Rabindranath Tagore

7. Who won the Nobel Prize in Physics in the same year Karl Landsteiner won the Nobel Prize in Physiology or Medicine?
   a) Albert Einstein
   b) C.V. Raman
   c) Niels Bohr
   d) Guglielmo Marconi

8. A maximum of how many people are allowed to share a Nobel Prize?
a) Two
b) Three
c) Four
d) Thirteen

9. The 2011 Nobel Peace Prize was shared by three women. If two were from Liberia, which country was the third person from?
a) United States
b) Yemen
c) China
d) Pakistan

10. In which category have both Marie Curie and Irène Curie won the Nobel Prize?
a) Medicine
b) Literature
c) Peace
d) Chemistry

11. The blue colour of the Mediterranean Sea inspired whom to discover his Nobel Prize-winning theory?
a) C.V. Raman
b) Isaac Newton
c) S. Ramanujan
d) Albert Einstein

12. In 1923, Frederick G. Banting and John Macleod received the Nobel Prize in Physiology or Medicine for the discovery of . . .
a) Insulin
b) Penicillin
c) Smallpox vaccine
d) Blood groups

13. In which category has the Nobel Prize been awarded the least number of times?
a) Physics
b) Peace
c) Medicine
d) Economic Sciences

14. Alfred Nobel incorporated nitroglycerine into silica and patented it under the name of . . .
a) Nuclear bomb
b) Laughing gas
c) Artificial limb
d) Dynamite

15. Who was the first American President to win the Nobel Peace Prize?
a) Theodore Roosevelt
b) John F. Kennedy
c) Jimmy Carter
d) Barack Obama

16. The prize in which category has been awarded by the Norwegian Nobel Committee since 1901?
a) Chemistry

b) Economic Sciences
c) Peace
d) Literature

17. Who received the Nobel Prize for Medicine in 1905 for his discoveries in relation to tuberculosis?
a) Alexander Fleming
b) Ronald Ross
c) Robert Koch
d) Louis Pasteur

18. Who among the following was the nephew of C.V. Raman?
a) Har Gobind Khorana
b) S. Chandrasekhar
c) Homi Bhabha
d) Jagadish Chandra Bose

19. Which organization has been honoured by the Nobel Peace Prize three times?
a) International Labour Organization
b) Amnesty International
c) United Nations
d) International Committee of the Red Cross

20. Which Nobel laureate wrote articles under the name Gul Makai?
a) Nadine Gordimer
b) Doris Lessing
c) Rigoberta Menchú Tum
d) Malala Yousafzai

NUMBERS

1. In Roman numerals, what does 'XL' stand for?
   a) Thirty
   b) Forty
   c) Fifty
   d) Sixty

2. Which of these values is equal to 10 lakh?
   a) 1 million
   b) 10 million
   c) 100 million
   d) 1 billion

3. How many sides does a dodecagon have?
   a) Three
   b) Twelve
   c) Seventeen
   d) Thirty

4. Which of these is an Indian word for one hundred lakh?
   a) Crore
   b) Million
   c) Arab
   d) Kharab

5. If you were writing 1 to 100 in words, how many times would you use the letter 'C'?
   a) Never
   b) Two
   c) Twenty-three
   d) 100

6. How many zeroes would you write after one, if you had to write one crore in numerals?
   a) Two
   b) Five
   c) Six
   d) Seven

7. How many zeros must you add to the number 100 to reach 10 lakh?
   a) Four
   b) Five
   c) Eight
   d) Ten

8. What is the number of thousand-rupee notes you would need in India to become a crorepati?
   a) 100
   b) Thousand

c) Ten thousand
d) One lakh

9. The word 'quarantine' comes from the Italian words quaranta giorni meaning . . .
a) Forty days
b) Fifty days
c) Sixty days
d) Eighty days

10. If you subtract hundred lakh from one crore, what would you be left with?
a) Nothing
b) Ten thousand
c) One lakh
d) One million

11. How many 5 rupee coins do you need to make 2 lakh rupees?
a) 4000
b) 40,000
c) 4 lakh
d) 40 lakh

12. Which mathematical sign was introduced by Robert Recorde in 1557?
a) Equals sign
b) Plus sign
c) Minus sign
d) Percentage sign

13. Which word would you use to describe a period of thousand years?
a) Decade
b) Millennium
c) Century
d) Jubilee

14. Which of these words refers to a score of zero?
a) Pigeon
b) Duck
c) Sparrow
d) Crow

15. What is the total number of dots on a dice?
a) Fourteen
b) Twenty-one
c) Twenty-six
d) Thirty-two

16. The Greek prefix hepta- refers to which number?
a) Six
b) Seven
c) Eight
d) Nine

17. In the Gregorian calendar, which is the last month to have thirty days?
a) August
b) October
c) November
d) December

18. The sixtieth anniversary of an important event is celebrated as...
a) Silver jubilee
b) Golden jubilee
c) Diamond jubilee
d) Ruby jubilee

19. How much is a baker's dozen?
a) Ten
b) Eleven
c) Twelve
d) Thirteen

20. Triskaidekaphobia is the irrational fear of the number ...
a) Three
b) Thirteen
c) Thirty
d) Fifty-three

OLYMPIC GAMES

1. The 1964 Summer Olympics was the first Olympic Games held in Asia. Which city hosted it?
a) Seoul
b) Tokyo
c) Beijing
d) Jakarta

2. In terms of the number of days, what has been the maximum duration of the Olympic Games?
a) Sixteen
b) Eighteen
c) Twenty
d) Twenty-one

3. Which of these was introduced at the 1920 Antwerp Olympic Games?
a) Mascot

b) Olympic flag with five rings
c) Torch relay
d) Gold medals

4. At the London Olympics of 1908, the distance from Windsor Castle to the Royal Box in the Olympic Stadium was fixed for which event?
a) Triathlon
b) Marathon
c) Sailing
d) Swimming

5. Which Olympic sport takes place on a mat called tatami and the contest lasts for five minutes?
a) Karate
b) Taekwondo
c) Judo
d) Sumo

6. Which of these is not included in the Olympic triathlon?
a) Swimming
b) Running
c) Cycling
d) Shooting

7. Norman Pritchard was the first Indian to win an Olympic medal in 1900. In which sport did he compete?
a) Athletics
b) Swimming
c) Gymnastics
d) Wrestling

8. In which sport did India win a medal for the first time ever at the 2012 London Olympic Games?
a) Wrestling
b) Hockey
c) Shooting
d) Badminton

9. A black disc called puck, made of hard rubber, is used in which sport?
a) Water polo
b) Volleyball
c) Lacrosse
d) Ice hockey

10. What is the 'shot' in the Olympic sport shot-put?
a) Hammer
b) Javelin
c) Metal ring
d) Metal ball

11. Which is the oldest of equestrian sports?
a) Eventing
b) Polo
c) Dressage
d) Jumping

12. In which sport did Nisha Millet represent India at the Sydney Olympics in 2000?
a) Weightlifting
b) Swimming

c) Hockey
d) Tennis

13. Which was the oldest sport at the Olympic Winter Games?
a) Ice hockey
b) Figure skating
c) Ski jumping
d) Luge

14. Which sport, last played at the 1904 Summer Olympics, was reintroduced after 112 years at the 2016 Rio Olympics?
a) Basketball
b) Badminton
c) Golf
d) Cricket

15. Who was India's first-ever individual Olympic gold medalist?
a) Rajyavardhan Singh Rathore
b) Vijay Kumar
c) Abhinav Bindra
d) P.V. Sindhu

16. Why were the 1916 Olympic Games, scheduled to be held in Berlin, cancelled?
a) World War I
b) Death of Max Müller
c) Sinking of the *Titanic*
d) An Atlantic hurricane

17. Swedish shooter Oscar Swahn won a silver medal in the team running deer-shooting, double shot event to become the . . .
a) Youngest medallist ever
b) First medallist from the United States
c) Oldest medallist ever
d) First medallist

18. In which sport are Greco-Roman and freestyle events held?
a) Wrestling
b) Fencing
c) Athletics
d) Boxing

19. Which country has won the most number of Winter Olympic medals?
a) South Korea
b) Norway
c) Switzerland
d) Germany

20. Having borrowed it from Henri Didon, his friend and a Dominican priest who taught sport, Pierre de Coubertin proposed the . . .
a) Olympic torch
b) Olympic flag
c) Olympic motto
d) Olympic creed

PLACES TO SEE

1. The idea for which monument was proposed by Édouard de Laboulaye?
   a) Statue of Liberty
   b) Eiffel Tower
   c) Sydney Opera House
   d) Golden Gate Bridge

2. At the base of which monument is the memorial Amar Jawan Jyoti?
   a) Gateway of India
   b) India Gate
   c) Shaheed Minar
   d) Red Fort

3. Which building, designed by British architect Edwin Lutyens, is located at Raisina Hill in New Delhi?
   a) Lotus Temple

b) Teen Murti Bhavan
c) Rashtrapati Bhavan
d) India Gate

4. Which structure did Guy de Maupassant ridicule as a 'high and skinny pyramid of iron ladders'?
a) Statue of Liberty
b) Leaning Tower of Pisa
c) Eiffel Tower
d) Sphinx

5. Which of the following monuments is the mausoleum of Muhammad Adil Shah?
a) Gol Gumbaz
b) Taj Mahal
c) Qutub Minar
d) Mohalla Bulbuli Khana

6. What was built by Sawai Jai Singh II in New Delhi, Jaipur, Ujjain, Varanasi and Mathura?
a) Hawa Mahal
b) Jantar Mantar
c) Amer Fort
d) Neemrana Fort

7. In the mid-eighteenth century, French Commander Bussy made which landmark in Hyderabad his home?
a) Salar Jung Museum
b) Golconda Fort
c) Amer Fort
d) Charminar

8. Which monument is painted every seven years with approximately 60 tonnes of paint?
   a) Qutub Minar
   b) Taj Mahal
   c) Eiffel Tower
   d) Great Wall of China

9. Which of these was not built by Shah Jahan?
   a) Red Fort
   b) Taj Mahal
   c) Jama Masjid
   d) Qutub Minar

10. Which was the first monument from Rajasthan to appear on the list of UNESCO World Heritage Sites?
   a) M.P. Birla Planetarium
   b) Vijay Stambh
   c) Taj Mahal
   d) Jantar Mantar

11. In 1869, Auguste Bartholdi designed a statue of a woman with a torch, named 'Egypt Carrying the Light to Asia' as a lighthouse for the Suez Canal. When this project failed, which famous structure did he complete in 1886?
   a) Eiffel Tower
   b) Statue of Liberty
   c) Leaning Tower of Pisa
   d) Pietà

12. The Nalanda Suite and the Marble Hall are parts of which building situated in New Delhi?
a) Red Fort
b) Parliament House
c) Qutub Minar
d) Rashtrapati Bhavan

13. Locally known as Verul Leni in Maharashtra, how do we better know these caves?
a) The Rock Shelters of Bhimbetka
b) Ellora Caves
c) Elephanta Caves
d) Ajanta Caves

14. If Shah Jahan built the Taj Mahal, what did Hamida Banu Begum build?
a) Gol Gumbaz
b) Diwan-i-Khas
c) Victoria Memorial
d) Humayun's Tomb

15. Which monument was built by Aurangzeb's son as a tribute to his mother Rabia Durrani?
a) Hawa Mahal
b) Bibi Ka Maqbara
c) Bara Imambara
d) Gol Gumbaz

16. In which continent are the pyramids of Giza located?
a) Asia
b) Europe

c) Africa
d) Australia

17. If you were visiting the famous Mehrangarh Fort, which state would you be in?
a) Gujarat
b) Rajasthan
c) Maharashtra
d) Odisha

18. How many storeys does the Hawa Mahal have?
a) One
b) Four
c) Five
d) Twenty

19. Which monument are you most likely to see from the Sireh Deori Bazaar?
a) Hawa Mahal
b) Charminar
c) Qutub Minar
d) Gol Gumbaz

20. At which landmark would you find the tombs of Akbarabadi Begum and Fatehpuri Begum, two of Shah Jahan's wives?
a) Taj Mahal
b) Humayun's Tomb
c) Charminar
d) Red Fort

POLITICS

1. In the 1990s, which Indian prime minister once lost to Vijay Kumar Malhotra in a parliamentary election?
   a) Manmohan Singh
   b) Rajiv Gandhi
   c) Indira Gandhi
   d) Lal Bahadur Shastri

2. Who was the first chairman of the Rajya Sabha to serve for two terms?
   a) S. Radhakrishnan
   b) Jawaharlal Nehru
   c) Vallabhbhai Patel
   d) B.R. Ambedkar

3. Who was the first Indian President to visit the world's highest battlefield, the Siachen Glacier?
   a) Pratibha Patil

b) A.P.J. Abdul Kalam
c) Pranab Mukherjee
d) No one has

4. Which Indian prime minister was born in Mughalsarai, Uttar Pradesh?
a) Lal Bahadur Shastri
b) Morarji Desai
c) Indira Gandhi
d) Rajiv Gandhi

5. Veer Bhoomi is the memorial to which Indian prime minister?
a) Indira Gandhi
b) Rajiv Gandhi
c) Jawaharlal Nehru
d) Lal Bahadur Shastri

6. In 1937, which Indian prime minister wrote an essay in the *Modern Review*, published in Calcutta (now Kolkata) under the pen name Chanakya?
a) Lal Bahadur Shastri
b) Indira Gandhi
c) Jawaharlal Nehru
d) P.V. Narasimha Rao

7. In India, what was reduced after the enactment of the Sixty-first Amendment Act?
a) The number of states in India
b) Voting age
c) High courts
d) National holidays

8. Mahatma Gandhi once sent Henry Ford an autographed version of . . .
a) The English translation of the Bhagavad Gita
b) A charkha
c) A khadi shawl
d) His walking stick

9. Which north Indian city is the birthplace of three Indian prime ministers?
a) Prayagraj
b) Jammu
c) Jaipur
d) Bathinda

10. V.V. Giri, F.A. Ahmed and N. Sanjiva Reddy were all . . .
a) Prime ministers of India
b) Presidents of India
c) Chief Election Commissioners
d) Governors of RBI

11. Who was the first serving President of India to cast a vote in a general election?
a) N. Sanjiva Reddy
b) K.R. Narayanan
c) Giani Zail Singh
d) Zakir Hussain

12. The Rashtrapati Bhavan in New Delhi was the erstwhile residence of the British . . .
a) Governor general
b) Viceroy

c) Prime minister
d) Queen

13. What is the minimum age required to be a member of the Rajya Sabha?
   a) Twenty years
   b) Thirty years
   c) Forty years
   d) Fifty years

14. In India, which of these posts has never been held by a woman?
   a) The President
   b) The vice president
   c) The prime minister
   d) The chief minister of a state

15. In 1945, which President, while working as a journalist, interviewed Mahatma Gandhi?
   a) Giani Zail Singh
   b) Jawaharlal Nehru
   c) K.R. Narayanan
   d) Pratibha Patil

16. In India, which ministry provides passports for citizens?
   a) Ministry of Railways
   b) Ministry of Textiles
   c) Ministry of Civil Aviation
   d) Ministry of External Affairs

17. The national legislative assembly of Sweden is known as the...
a) Riksdag
b) Knesset
c) Seimas
d) Congress

18. In 1966, who was sworn in as the acting prime minister of India after the death of Lal Bahadur Shastri in Tashkent?
a) Manmohan Singh
b) Gulzarilal Nanda
c) B.R. Ambedkar
d) Morarji Desai

19. Who was the first vice president of India to become president?
a) Rajendra Prasad
b) S. Radhakrishnan
c) V.V. Giri
d) N. Sanjiva Reddy

20. Till date, who has been the youngest prime minister of India?
a) Lal Bahadur Shastri
b) Chaudhary Charan Singh
c) Morarji Desai
d) Rajiv Gandhi

SCIENCE

1. Which instrument's name comes from two Greek words meaning 'chest' and 'to explore'?
a) Stethoscope
b) Barometer
c) Thermometer
d) Pacemaker

2. As it takes less fuel to launch a spacecraft in lower gravity, most bases are located near the . . .
a) Tropic of Cancer
b) Prime meridian
c) Equator
d) South Pole

3. If oxygen supply is high, the colour of a flame appears . . .
a) Blue
b) Yellow

c) Red
d) Green

4. Which of these elements is named after a Swedish city?
a) Strontium
b) Holmium
c) Berkelium
d) Polonium

5. If 'S' stands for Single and 'L' stands for Lens, what does 'R' in SLR stand for?
a) Record
b) Reprography
c) Reflex
d) Rotation

6. Following the accidental melting of a chocolate, what did Percy Spencer invent?
a) Pressure cooker
b) Microwave oven
c) Refrigerator
d) Vacuum cleaner

7. Which of these words comes from two Greek words meaning 'alongside' and 'food'?
a) Virus
b) Bacteria
c) Parasite
d) Protein

8. With the help of which natural phenomenon was Albert Einstein's general theory of relativity proved?
a) Rainbow
b) Total solar eclipse
c) Mirage
d) Tsunami

9. Whose birth anniversary is celebrated as National Statistics Day in India?
a) P.C. Mahalanobis
b) C.V. Raman
c) S. Ramanujan
d) Satish Dhawan

10. In Albert Einstein's famous equation $E=mc^2$, the letter 'c' denotes the speed of ...
a) Wind
b) Waves
c) Light
d) Sound

11. Which scientist set up the Volta Laboratory, an institution devoted to studying deafness?
a) Thomas Edison
b) Nikola Tesla
c) Alexander Graham Bell
d) Humphry Davy

12. In 1896, who gave up German citizenship and was not a citizen of any country until 1901?
a) Adolf Hitler

b) Karl Marx
c) Albert Einstein
d) Vladimir Lenin

13. Along with Y.S. Rajan, who wrote the book *India 2020: A Vision for the New Millennium*?
a) A.P.J. Abdul Kalam
b) C.N.R. Rao
c) Homi Bhabha
d) Satish Dhawan

14. Which of these boils at around 2700°C and melts at around 1063°C?
a) Cadmium
b) Gold
c) Helium
d) Mercury

15. The element with the chemical symbol Es is named after . . .
a) Albert Einstein
b) Thomas Edison
c) Ernest Rutherford
d) Ernest Hemingway

16. Which of these elements is named after a country?
a) Curium
b) Indium
c) Francium
d) Osmium

17. Which of these scientific units is not named after a person?
   a) Hertz
   b) Pascal
   c) Candela
   d) Watt

18. The name of which ancient branch of Indian medicine means 'knowledge of life' in Sanskrit?
   a) Ayurveda
   b) Homeopathy
   c) Reiki
   d) Acupuncture

19. Which of these gases is commonly used to disinfect water and is part of the sanitation process for sewage and industrial waste?
   a) Ammonia
   b) Hydrogen
   c) Chlorine
   d) Helium

20. According to Albert Einstein, '_____ is more important than knowledge.' Fill in the blank.
   a) Education
   b) Learning
   c) Imagination
   d) Intelligence

SPORTS I

1. In 2016, who became the first male tennis player to win 300 Grand Slam singles matches in the Open Era?
   a) Novak Djokovic
   b) Roger Federer
   c) Rafael Nadal
   d) Andy Murray

2. How many types of coloured cards can be shown in a game of field hockey?
   a) Six
   b) Four
   c) Three
   d) Two

3. Vivekananda Yuba Bharati Krirangan in Kolkata is the home ground of which franchise in the Indian Super League?
   a) Jamshedpur FC

b) Chennaiyin FC
c) ATK Mohun Bagan FC
d) Kerala Blasters FC

4. Whose autobiography is titled *Playing to Win*?
   a) Sania Mirza
   b) P.T. Usha
   c) Jhulan Goswami
   d) Saina Nehwal

5. In which sport would a player use techniques like hook, jab and uppercut?
   a) Boxing
   b) Shooting
   c) Karate
   d) Judo

6. What is the national sport of Bangladesh?
   a) Cricket
   b) Kabaddi
   c) Football
   d) Kho-kho

7. In an international football match, if a player is in his own half, which of these is true?
   a) Can handle the ball
   b) Can stop a player by hand
   c) Cannot be ruled offside
   d) Cannot be given a red card

8. Which chess player's rapid playing speed earned him/her the nickname 'the Lightning Kid'?
a) Viswanathan Anand
b) Koneru Humpy
c) Surya Sekhar Ganguly
d) Tania Sachdev

9. In 1972, which colour was introduced for tennis balls so as to make them more visible on television?
a) Pink
b) Yellow
c) Black
d) Orange

10. Which Indian state is known for the martial art form Kalaripayattu?
a) Tamil Nadu
b) Kerala
c) Karnataka
d) Maharashtra

11. Which is the only Grand Slam tennis tournament to have been played on three surfaces: grass, clay and hard court?
a) Australian Open
b) US Open
c) Wimbledon
d) French Open

12. The Premier League started in 1992–93. Which team won the title in the inaugural year?
a) Manchester United

b) Newcastle United
c) Arsenal
d) Blackburn Rovers

13. Which of these sportspersons has not had a biopic based on him/her?
a) M.C. Mary Kom
b) Milkha Singh
c) P.T. Usha
d) Paan Singh Tomar

14. Who was the first badminton player from India to win an Olympic medal?
a) Saina Nehwal
b) P.V. Sindhu
c) P. Gopichand
d) Prakash Padukone

15. Ken Aston, a football referee, was inspired by traffic lights to start which one of the following?
a) Yellow and red cards
b) Different coloured jerseys
c) Red and green footballs
d) Goalposts

16. Which tournament was originally known as the International Lawn Tennis Challenge Trophy?
a) Wimbledon
b) Davis Cup
c) French Open
d) Indian Wells Masters

17. In 2005, who became India's first Formula One racing driver?
a) Arjun Maini
b) Kamui Kobayashi
c) Narain Karthikeyan
d) Karun Chandhok

18. Which of these is not a card shown during a hockey match?
a) Red card
b) Green card
c) Yellow card
d) Blue card

19. Who was the first Asian player to win a Grand Slam singles title?
a) Naomi Osaka
b) Peng Shuai
c) Li Na
d) Ayumi Morita

20. Friedrich Ludwig Jahn is often referred to as the father of which sport?
a) Wrestling
b) Formula One
c) Gymnastics
d) Boxing

SPORTS II

1. With which sport would you associate Deepika Kumari, Bombayla Devi Laishram and Laxmirani Majhi?
   a) Archery
   b) Badminton
   c) Volleyball
   d) Swimming

2. Who wrote *Serve to Win: The 14-Day Gluten-Free Plan for Physical and Mental Excellence?*
   a) Andre Agassi
   b) Novak Djokovic
   c) Roger Federer
   d) Viswanathan Anand

3. The attacker in kabaddi is also known as the . . .
   a) Robber
   b) Raider

c) Burglar

d) Dacoit

4. Whose signature stance is called the 'To Di World' pose?
   a) Cristiano Ronaldo
   b) Usain Bolt
   c) Mo Farah
   d) Michael Phelps

5. In chess, which piece combines the regular moving abilities of a rook and a bishop?
   a) King
   b) Knight
   c) Pawn
   d) Queen

6. In which of these sports is a red card not shown?
   a) Football
   b) Hockey
   c) Table tennis
   d) Billiards

7. After which of these inventors was the footballer Pele named?
   a) Thomas Edison
   b) George Stephenson
   c) Benjamin Franklin
   d) Nikola Tesla

8. The triathlon comprises swimming, running and …
   a) Cycling
   b) Skiing

c) Sailing
d) Driving

9. Yubi Lakpi is the traditional sport of Manipur. What do the
    words mean in the local language?
    a) Coconut snatching
    b) Sword fight
    c) Bullseye
    d) Hitting the jackpot

10. In which city is the FIFA headquarters located?
    a) Zurich
    b) Madrid
    c) Milan
    d) London

11. Which sport is called *bhavatik* in Maldives and *sadugudu* in
    Tamil Nadu?
    a) Kho-kho
    b) Kabaddi
    c) Rugby
    d) Mallakhamb

12. Who has been the highest scorer in the history of FC
    Barcelona?
    a) Ronaldinho
    b) Lionel Messi
    c) Neymar Jr
    d) Cesc Fàbregas

13. Which game is sometimes called ping-pong?
   a) Polo
   b) Hockey
   c) Table tennis
   d) Basketball

14. What is the traditional colour of the jersey of the Indian national football team?
   a) Blue
   b) Green
   c) Orange
   d) Red

15. Among these, which boxing category is the heaviest?
   a) Flyweight
   b) Bantamweight
   c) Featherweight
   d) Minimum weight

16. After which sportsperson is Madeira Airport named?
   a) Tiger Woods
   b) Sachin Tendulkar
   c) Michael Phelps
   d) Cristiano Ronaldo

17. With which sport would you associate Maninder Singh, Siddharth Desai and Pardeep Narwal?
   a) Kabaddi
   b) Wrestling
   c) Badminton
   d) Golf

18. Which sportsperson sang the music singles 'Champion' and 'Run D World'?
   a) Brett Lee
   b) Dwayne Bravo
   c) Serena Williams
   d) Anna Kournikova

19. Whose autobiography is titled *Unbreakable*?
   a) P.T. Usha
   b) P.V. Sindhu
   c) M.C. Mary Kom
   d) Mithali Raj

20. In the history of the FIFA World Cup, Lucien Laurent of France was the first player to . . .
   a) Be red-carded
   b) Get injured
   c) Score a goal
   d) Referee a match

TECHNOLOGY

1. With which of these applications is the phrase 'last seen' most commonly associated?
   a) YouTube
   b) WhatsApp
   c) Instagram
   d) Twitter

2. What did the first webcam in the world show?
   a) A coffee pot
   b) A computer
   c) A traffic jam
   d) An apple

3. Who is credited with the invention of television?
   a) John Logie Baird
   b) Thomas Edison

c) Nikola Tesla
d) Johannes Gutenberg

4. When we talk about UI in smartphones, we are referring to the . . .
a) User interface
b) Uninterrupted service
c) Ultra intelligence
d) Usage instructions

5. Who invented the magnetic credit card strip in 1968?
a) Eli Whitney
b) Samuel O'Reilly
c) Ron Klein
d) Rudolf Diesel

6. Till 2016, which country had the largest number of mobile phone users?
a) India
b) Mozambique
c) Brazil
d) China

7. In 1839, Robert Cornelius, an amateur chemist, is said to have created the world's first . . .
a) Instant message
b) Tweet
c) Selfie
d) Blog

8. Which video game includes characters like Scarlett Fox and Montana Smith?
a) Candy Crush Saga
b) Temple Run
c) Subway Surfers
d) Fruit Ninja

9. What is a unit of information equal to 1,048,576 bytes called?
a) Gigabyte
b) Megabyte
c) Terabyte
d) Kilobyte

10. Chris Messina, a former designer at Google, proposed which symbol for Twitter that was earlier known as the 'pound symbol'?
a) Double ticks
b) Hashtag
c) The @ sign
d) Like

11. Till 2016, which language was used by the most number of internet users?
a) Hindi
b) English
c) Spanish
d) Japanese

12. Which of the following would you find on the logo of the application Instagram?
a) A hummingbird

b) A lightning bolt
c) A clock
d) A camera

13. In 2003, METSAT or India's meteorological series of satellites, was renamed after whom?
a) Rakesh Sharma
b) Kalpana Chawla
c) Edmund Hillary
d) Arundhati Roy

14. .af is the internet code of which country?
a) Angola
b) Australia
c) Afghanistan
d) Bhutan

15. Which video game features ghosts such as Blinky, Inky, Pinky and Clyde?
a) Subway Surfers
b) Temple Run
c) Candy Crush Saga
d) Pac-Man

16. In Twitter, what do the letters 'RT' stand for?
a) Real Tweet
b) Runtime
c) Retweet
d) Repeat Tweet

17. Which was the first YouTube video to hit more than one billion likes?
   a) Obama's victory speech
   b) Usain Bolt's 100 m sprint
   c) Curiosity's video from Mars
   d) PSY's 'Gangnam Style'

18. The official name of the Twitter bird is . . .
   a) Sandy
   b) Larry
   c) Jordan
   d) Jack

19. On 6 August 1991, who published the first-ever website while working at CERN?
   a) Albert Einstein
   b) Tim Berners-Lee
   c) Mark Zuckerberg
   d) Bill Gates

20. The woofer and the tweeter are different types of . . .
   a) Printers
   b) Washing machines
   c) Loudspeakers
   d) Refrigerator

TRAVEL

1. In 2006, the governor of Karnataka was requested to rename the Chennai–Mysore train service as ...
   a) Maratha Express
   b) Malgudi Express
   c) Coffee Express
   d) Vidhana Soudha Express

2. When travelling from north to south in India, which of the following places will you reach last?
   a) Patna
   b) Darjeeling
   c) Panaji
   d) Nagpur

3. In which Indian state is Biju Patnaik International Airport located?
   a) West Bengal

b) Odisha
c) Madhya Pradesh
d) Punjab

4. After which famous person is the SSPN railway station at Puttaparthi named?
   a) Sri Aurobindo
   b) Indira Gandhi
   c) M.S. Dhoni
   d) Sathya Sai Baba

5. The originating station of Chetak Express is Delhi. Which is its last stop?
   a) Meerut
   b) Udaipur
   c) Jhansi
   d) Jaipur

6. In which neighbouring country of India would you find the Pashupatinath Temple?
   a) Bangladesh
   b) Nepal
   c) Afghanistan
   d) China

7. Which of these monuments is located in a state capital?
   a) Gol Gumbaz
   b) Charminar
   c) Meenakshi Temple
   d) Golden Temple

8. The originating station of Vivek Express is Dibrugarh in Assam. Which is its last stop?
   a) Madurai
   b) Mumbai
   c) Udhampur
   d) Kanyakumari

9. If you landed at Sardar Vallabhbhai Patel International Airport, which of these cities would you be in?
   a) New Delhi
   b) Mumbai
   c) Chennai
   d) Ahmedabad

10. If you were visiting the Kachari Ruins and Dzukou Valley, which state would you be in?
   a) Maharashtra
   b) Uttar Pradesh
   c) Bihar
   d) Nagaland

11. After which former law minister of India is the international airport at Nagpur named?
   a) B.R. Ambedkar
   b) Maulana Azad
   c) Mahatma Gandhi
   d) Rajendra Prasad

12. The luxury train Deccan Odyssey is a joint venture between Indian Railways and the government of . . .
   a) Tamil Nadu

b) Odisha

c) Maharashtra

d) Uttar Pradesh

13. If you are travelling by Indian Railways with the ticket code 'CC', then you are travelling in . . .

a) AC 2 Tier

b) AC Chair Car

c) First Class

d) Sleeper Class

14. The name of which train means 'non-stop' or 'quick' in Bengali?

a) Rajdhani

b) Shatabdi

c) Duronto

d) Garib Rath

15. In Indian Railways, what does the class code 'SL' stand for?

a) Special

b) Sleeper

c) Slow

d) Single

16. What is the source station of the Akal Takht Express?

a) Amritsar

b) Dwarka

c) Patna

d) Puri

17. In which state is the Nashik Kumbh Mela held?

a) Kerala

b) Maharashtra
c) Odisha
d) Tamil Nadu

18. Which city is served by Chaudhary Charan Singh International Airport?
a) Patna
b) Dehradun
c) Lucknow
d) Raipur

19. What is the minimum age you need to be to get an Indian passport?
a) 15 years
b) 18 years
c) 21 years
d) None

20. In which city is the Jolly Grant Airport located?
a) Panaji
b) Jaipur
c) Dehradun
d) Chennai

WILDLIFE I

1. A species of which bird is the fastest underwater swimming bird?
   a) Penguin
   b) Pelican
   c) Kingfisher
   d) Hummingbird

2. What is the colour of an octopus's blood?
   a) Blue
   b) Green
   c) Red
   d) Yellow

3. Which country is the breeding ground of 60 per cent of the world's Atlantic puffins?
   a) Iceland
   b) Canada

c) Nepal

d) Brazil

4. Which bird was once known as the 'camel bird' because of its long neck?

a) Pelican

b) Crane

c) Ostrich

d) Albatross

5. Which bird from the sword-billed species has the longest bill of any bird relative to its body length?

a) Crane

b) Kingfisher

c) Pelican

d) Hummingbird

6. What makes the African pygmy squirrel special?

a) It is the smallest squirrel.

b) It is the heaviest squirrel.

c) It is the largest squirrel.

d) It is the largest mammal.

7. Which of these animals does not have spots on its body?

a) Giraffe

b) Chital

c) Sangai

d) Dalmatian

8. Of these four breeds of dogs, which is the tallest?

a) Pug

b) Great Dane
c) Labrador
d) Irish wolfhound

9. In India, what do the Changra and Chegu breeds of goat produce?
a) Pashmina
b) Merino wool
c) Silk
d) Velvet

10. *Macropus giganteus*, meaning 'big foot', is the scientific name of which of these animals?
a) Kangaroo
b) Giraffe
c) Giant panda
d) Zebra

11. Which is the only big cat that can turn mid-air while following its prey?
a) Lion
b) Leopard
c) Cheetah
d) Jaguar

12. Which is the only bird that has its nostrils at the end of its bill?
a) Kingfisher
b) Kiwi
c) Crow
d) Pelican

13. Sahiwal, Ongole, Red Sindhi and Jersey are different breeds of which animal?
a) Goats
b) Horses
c) Blue whales
d) Cows

14. Which is the heaviest living bird in the world?
a) Hummingbird
b) Ostrich
c) Crane
d) Albatross

15. Which of these has the lowest body temperature of any bird?
a) Ostrich
b) Hummingbird
c) Kiwi
d) Penguin

16. Which animal is called *ora* or 'land crocodile' by the locals in Indonesia?
a) Giant panda
b) Komodo dragon
c) King cobra
d) Chimpanzee

17. A shrimp's heart is located in its ...
a) Head
b) Legs
c) Hands
d) Liver

18. Which of these creatures does not have a circulatory system?
a) Hippopotamus
b) Jellyfish
c) Frog
d) Shark

19. Black mambas get their name from the blue-black colour of ...
a) Their pupils
b) Their skin
c) The insides of their mouth
d) Their fangs

20. Which is the only mammal that survives by consuming blood?
a) Vampire bat
b) Mongoose
c) Polar bear
d) Chimpanzee

WILDLIFE II

1. The tail of which of these creatures can break off and regenerate?
   a) Cat
   b) Iguana
   c) Elephant
   d) Rabbit

2. Which animal is the source of a vast majority of human rabies cases?
   a) Cows
   b) Sheep
   c) Cats
   d) Dogs

3. Which of these is not a reptile?
   a) Gecko
   b) Savannah monitor

c) Salamander
d) Terrapin

4. What does an emperor penguin normally keep in a 'brood pouch'?
a) Stones
b) Fish
c) Snowflakes
d) Eggs

5. The lower half of the bill of which bird can hold about 11 litres of water, which is more than can be held in its stomach?
a) Pelican
b) Crane
c) Flamingo
d) Albatross

6. At about 6 feet, which animal's legs are taller than many human beings?
a) Zebra
b) Hippopotamus
c) Giraffe
d) Bulldog

7. Which breed of dog can run the fastest?
a) Afghan hound
b) Greyhound
c) Dobermann
d) Basset hound

8. Funnel-web, redback and brown recluse are different species of . . .
a) Ants
b) Spiders
c) Snakes
d) Turtles

9. Which member of the cat family appears on the state emblem of India?
a) Tiger
b) Cheetah
c) Lion
d) Puma

10. Which part of an enemy's body does the spitting cobra of Africa aim at?
a) Eyes
b) Neck
c) Feet
d) Ears

11. Which is the only bird to have just two toes on each foot?
a) Penguin
b) Emu
c) Ostrich
d) Kiwi

12. Which of the following do not lay eggs?
a) Mosquitoes
b) Penguins

c) King cobras
d) Aardvarks

13. Which reptile gets its name from Greek words meaning 'terrible lizard'?
a) Chameleon
b) Dinosaur
c) Tuatara
d) Snake

14. Which of these big cats cannot roar?
a) Lion
b) Cheetah
c) Jaguar
d) Tiger

15. Which of these is the largest predatory fish in the world?
a) Dolphin
b) Blue whale
c) Great white shark
d) Swordfish

16. Fire, pharaoh, army and carpenter are different types of . . .
a) Spiders
b) Cockroaches
c) Ants
d) Bees

17. Which animal has the longest tail of all land mammals?
a) Kangaroo
b) Giraffe

c) Elephant
d) Zebra

18. Which animal's name comes from a native American word meaning 'he who kills with one leap'?
a) Bandicoot
b) Jaguar
c) Sloth
d) Coyote

19. Which of these is the tallest of all marsupials?
a) Kangaroos
b) Koalas
c) Wombats
d) Tasmanian devils

20. The scientific name of which animal has the suffix 'unicornis'?
a) Blackbuck
b) Indian rhinoceros
c) Hippopotamus
d) Musk deer

THE WORLD AROUND US

1. If you were eating xacuti, prawn balchão or bebinca, which state would you be in?
   a) Tripura
   b) Goa
   c) Himachal Pradesh
   d) Gujarat

2. What is the official religion of Cambodia?
   a) Buddhism
   b) Sikhism
   c) Jainism
   d) Zoroastrianism

3. Which feat connects James Irwin, David Scott and Alan Shepard?
   a) Climbing Mount Everest

b) Landing on the moon
c) Reaching North Pole
d) Discovering Antarctica

4. Which profession would you be in if you wore a toque?
   a) Doctor
   b) Lawyer
   c) Chef
   d) Policeman

5. With which country would you associate ikebana, the art of flower arrangement?
   a) Japan
   b) Germany
   c) Nepal
   d) Thailand

6. Where would you find the names of scientists Lavoisier, Ampere and Chevreul, in that order?
   a) Leaning Tower of Pisa
   b) Eiffel Tower
   c) The Statue of Liberty
   d) Stonehenge

7. Kuchipudi is indigenous to which state of India?
   a) Kerala
   b) Andhra Pradesh
   c) Odisha
   d) Tamil Nadu

8. With which state in India would you associate Warli folk paintings?
a) Maharashtra
b) Gujarat
c) Rajasthan
d) Karnataka

9. What are log, yearner, soldier, freefall and starfish types of?
a) Fictional warriors
b) Cakes
c) Moustaches
d) Sleeping positions

10. Who signs the Bharat Ratna certificate?
a) Prime minister of India
b) President of India
c) No one
d) Chief Justice of India

11. Apart from white, what is the official colour of Canada?
a) Yellow
b) Red
c) Orange
d) Blue

12. Who were the first Indian couple to feature on an Indian postage stamp after independence?
a) Mahatma and Kasturba Gandhi
b) Jawaharlal and Kamala Nehru
c) Sachin and Anjali Tendulkar
d) No one

13. In which state are the most number of jute mills located?
   a) West Bengal
   b) Kerala
   c) Assam
   d) Bihar

14. Which country's national anthem is 'Marcha Real'?
   a) United States
   b) Spain
   c) Bangladesh
   d) United Kingdom

15. In which of these countries was television introduced in 1999?
   a) United States
   b) UAE
   c) Bhutan
   d) Bangladesh

16. Natural teak forests grow in Laos, Myanmar, Thailand and . . .
   a) China
   b) Sri Lanka
   c) India
   d) Japan

17. What does 'L' stand for in the abbreviation ILO?
   a) Legal
   b) Labour
   c) Literary
   d) Livelihood

18. Arches, whorls, radial loops and ulnar loops are patterns of ...
   a) Leaves
   b) Fingerprints
   c) Sand dunes
   d) Corals

19. Sherpas are known for their skill in ...
   a) Breeding camels
   b) Sword fighting
   c) Mountaineering
   d) Scuba diving

20. Who received the Nobel Peace Prize in 1919 for his efforts to create the League of Nations?
   a) Abraham Lincoln
   b) Theodore Roosevelt
   c) Ronald Reagan
   d) Woodrow Wilson

WORLD GEOGRAPHY I

1. Which of these means 'the land of the little sticks' in Russian?
   a) Taiga
   b) Savanna
   c) Steppes
   d) Tundra

2. Which is the most densely populated hot desert in the world?
   a) Sahara
   b) Namib
   c) Thar
   d) Gobi

3. According to the Guinness World Records, which is the world's lowest lying country?
   a) Germany

b) Sri Lanka
c) The Netherlands
d) Nepal

4. What are Harmattan, Sirocco and Mistral types of?
   a) Cyclones
   b) Tsunamis
   c) Winds
   d) Rivers

5. Which mountain range runs through seven South American countries?
   a) Atlas
   b) Andes
   c) Ural
   d) Alps

6. Which country's administrative centre is Putrajaya?
   a) Cambodia
   b) Malaysia
   c) Australia
   d) Sri Lanka

7. In which country would you find the Churia Range and the Mahabharat Range?
   a) Sri Lanka
   b) Pakistan
   c) Nepal
   d) Bangladesh

8. In which country would you get to see the 'Long Wall of Ten Thousand Li'?
a) China
b) Afghanistan
c) Japan
d) Thailand

9. Which of these states shares its border with Bangladesh?
a) Tripura
b) Andhra Pradesh
c) Madhya Pradesh
d) Maharashtra

10. Which river was referred to as the Aigyptos in Homer's *Odyssey*?
a) Volga
b) Danube
c) Nile
d) Ganga

11. In Japan, *goraiko* is a term reserved for . . .
a) The sunrise seen from Mount Fuji
b) The tea used in the tea ceremony
c) The longest river
d) The best samurai

12. A line on a map joining points of equal height, above or below sea level, is called a/an . . .
a) Contour line
b) Isohyet

c) Latitude

d) Isobar

13. Which continent has been inhabited for the longest period of time?

a) Africa

b) Antarctica

c) Uzbekistan

d) Australia

14. In which country is the UNESCO World Heritage Site Aapravasi Ghat situated?

a) Fiji

b) Mauritius

c) Sri Lanka

d) China

15. Which continent is classified as a desert?

a) Asia

b) Antarctica

c) Europe

d) North America

16. In which present-day country would you see the archaeological ruins of Mohenjo-Daro?

a) Pakistan

b) Sri Lanka

c) Bhutan

d) Nepal

17. Which country is home to the Sagarmatha National Park?
a) India
b) Sri Lanka
c) Bhutan
d) Nepal

18. Apart from India, with which country does Bangladesh share its land boundaries?
a) Myanmar
b) Pakistan
c) China
d) Russia

19. Which is the largest country in the world to have a single time zone?
a) Sri Lanka
b) China
c) Brazil
d) United States

20. An extensive group of islands is called an . . .
a) Archipelago
b) Aggradation
c) Atoll
d) Anticline

WORLD GEOGRAPHY II

1. In an atlas, which letter would Vietnam be shaped like?
a) V
b) S
c) T
d) X

2. Which continent has the longest coastline?
a) Australia
b) Africa
c) Europe
d) Asia

3. Around 60 per cent of the Sundarbans forest is in which country?
a) Nepal
b) Bangladesh

c) Sri Lanka
d) India

4. Which is the warmest and saltiest sea in the world?
a) Arctic Sea
b) Caspian Sea
c) Arabian Sea
d) Red Sea

5. The Palk Strait lies between India and which other country?
a) Bangladesh
b) Nepal
c) Pakistan
d) Sri Lanka

6. The summit of Mount Koussi in Chad is the highest point of which desert?
a) Sahara
b) Namib
c) Gobi
d) Kalahari

7. Which is the southernmost continent in the world?
a) Antarctica
b) Europe
c) Australia
d) Africa

8. Which of these capital cities is situated in Asia?
a) Cairo
b) Jakarta

c) Lima

d) Amsterdam

9. Which of these countries shares the shortest international boundary with India?

a) Nepal

b) China

c) Myanmar

d) Bhutan

10. Located at an altitude of 11,942 feet, which is the highest administrative capital city in the world?

a) La Paz

b) Sydney

c) Beijing

d) Brasilia

11. Which of these mountains forms the traditional boundary between Europe and Asia?

a) Ural

b) Atlas

c) Andes

d) Rockies

12. Which of these countries consists of a chain of about 1200 small coral islands on the Indian Ocean?

a) Thailand

b) Bangladesh

c) Afghanistan

d) Maldives

13. French Guiana, an overseas territorial collectivity of France, is located in which continent?
a) South America
b) Europe
c) Asia
d) Africa

14. Mount Kosciuszko is the highest mountain in ...
a) Europe
b) North America
c) Australia
d) South America

15. Luzon is the largest island of which Asian nation?
a) Philippines
b) Indonesia
c) Malaysia
d) Japan

16. Which neighbouring country of India is home to Kelani Ganga and Kalu Ganga?
a) Nepal
b) Sri Lanka
c) Bangladesh
d) Cambodia

17. Which is the only continent without glaciers?
a) Australia
b) Antarctica
c) Europe
d) Africa

18. The first aerial survey of which peak was done in 1933?
   a) Mount Everest
   b) Mount Fuji
   c) Mount Kilimanjaro
   d) K2

19. Which is the largest city in Iraq?
   a) Cairo
   b) Baghdad
   c) Mosul
   d) Karbala

20. The origin of which of these terms is jointly credited to Pierre Gassendi and Galileo Galilei?
   a) Aurora australis
   b) Aurora borealis
   c) Oasis
   d) Mirage

WORLD HISTORY I

1. Which of these had the birth name Rolihlahla, meaning 'troublemaker' in the language of the Xhosa tribe?
   a) Martin Luther King, Jr
   b) Nelson Mandela
   c) Barack Obama
   d) Winston Churchill

2. Which country is officially called Hellenic Republic?
   a) Hungary
   b) Spain
   c) Italy
   d) Greece

3. Which was the eighth month of the early Roman republican calendar?
   a) September
   b) October

c) November
d) December

4. Whose voyages of discovery have been immortalized in Portugal's patriotic poem, *The Lusiads*?
   a) Ibn Batuta
   b) Ferdinand Magellan
   c) Vasco da Gama
   d) Marco Polo

5. Who wrote the first volume of his autobiography in the Landsberg am Lech fortress?
   a) Nelson Mandela
   b) Anne Frank
   c) Benito Mussolini
   d) Adolf Hitler

6. Napoleon wanted to send 15,000 men to help a ruler fight the British. Name the ruler.
   a) Shivaji
   b) Rani Lakshmibai
   c) Prithviraj Chauhan
   d) Tipu Sultan

7. In 1987, the Italian government approved a $25 million project to prevent the _____ from tilting further. Fill in the blank.
   a) Leaning Tower of Pisa
   b) Statue of Liberty
   c) Eiffel Tower
   d) Sydney Opera House

8. Who was the monarch of Great Britain when India became independent?
   a) Queen Anne
   b) Queen Victoria
   c) King George VI
   d) Queen Elizabeth II

9. Who wrote *Sanitary Statistics of Native Colonial Schools and Hospitals*?
   a) Mother Teresa
   b) Florence Nightingale
   c) Joan of Arc
   d) Princess Diana

10. Who named more than seventy cities after himself, including one at the mouth of the Nile?
   a) Attila the Hun
   b) Napoleon
   c) Alexander the Great
   d) Julius Caesar

11. In 1893, which country's police force issued the world's first car number plates?
   a) United States
   b) Germany
   c) France
   d) Russia

12. The signing of which treaty officially ended World War I?
   a) Treaty of Warsaw
   b) Treaty of Bonn

c) Treaty of Versailles

d) Treaty of Alton

13. In 1919, who organized unemployed war veterans into armed squads known as the Blackshirts?

a) Che Guevara

b) Kim Jong Il

c) Benito Mussolini

d) Fulgencio Batista

14. Who, in Portugal, attempted to gain royal patronage for his 'enterprise of the Indies'?

a) Bartolomeu Dias

b) Christopher Columbus

c) Ferdinand Magellan

d) Vasco da Gama

15. Which month in the Gregorian calendar was named after the first Roman emperor?

a) July

b) August

c) October

d) May

16. What name, meaning 'bringer of light', was adopted by Nguyen Tat Thanh?

a) Che Guevara

b) Fidel Castro

c) Ho Chi Minh

d) Winston Churchill

17. Which of these names actually means 'splendour of dharma'?
  a) Fa-hsien
  b) Megasthenes
  c) Jean-Baptiste Tavernier
  d) Hiuen Tsang

18. Which historical character's favourite horse was Incitatus?
  a) Alexander
  b) Nelson
  c) Caligula
  d) Nero

19. Who gave the speech titled 'I Am Prepared to Die'?
  a) Mahatma Gandhi
  b) Nelson Mandela
  c) Martin Luther King, Jr
  d) Adolf Hitler

20. Which of these codes streamlined the French legal system and still continues to form the foundation of French civil law?
  a) Charlemagne's Code of Chivalry
  b) D'Artagnan Code
  c) Code of Voltaire
  d) Napoleonic Code

WORLD HISTORY II

1. In 1733, who published an almanac under the pen name Richard Saunders?
   a) Benjamin Franklin
   b) George Washington
   c) Abraham Lincoln
   d) Thomas Jefferson

2. By what spiritual name was Sehi, a Buddhist monk, popularly known?
   a) Xuanzang
   b) Fa-hsien
   c) Lao Tzu
   d) Confucius

3. Who was the first Englishman to circumnavigate the globe?
   a) Francis Drake
   b) Christopher Columbus

c) Ferdinand Magellan
d) Marco Polo

4. In which present-day country had Rama I established the Chakri dynasty?
   a) Thailand
   b) Japan
   c) Sri Lanka
   d) Nepal

5. The city of Orleans, associated with Joan of Arc, is located in . . .
   a) France
   b) United Kingdom
   c) Germany
   d) United States

6. Who was voted Time Magazine's Man of the Year in 1938?
   a) Che Guevara
   b) Fidel Castro
   c) Ho Chi Minh
   d) Adolf Hitler

7. Who is often referred to as Fakhr-e-Afghan?
   a) Shaukat Ali
   b) Maulana Azad
   c) Khan Abdul Ghaffar Khan
   d) Muhammad Ali Jinnah

8. Who was the sixteenth president of the United States?
   a) George Washington

b) Woodrow Wilson
c) Herbert Hoover
d) Abraham Lincoln

9. In which country did the Tiananmen Square protests take place?
a) Indonesia
b) Sri Lanka
c) China
d) Japan

10. Which US President had a team of advisers popularly known as the Brain Trust?
a) George Washington
b) Abraham Lincoln
c) Bill Clinton
d) Franklin Roosevelt

11. The Hundred Years War lasted for how many years?
a) 116
b) 120
c) Ninety-nine
d) Ninety

12. In 1907, who became the first woman to receive the Order of Merit in the UK?
a) Marie Curie
b) Mother Teresa
c) Florence Nightingale
d) Annie Besant

13. Which city was known as Edo until 1868?
a) Shanghai
b) Tokyo
c) Dhaka
d) Jakarta

14. Who was the US President when Neil Armstrong set foot on the moon?
a) Richard Nixon
b) John F. Kennedy
c) Abraham Lincoln
d) George W. Bush

15. Ivan IV, also known as Ivan the Terrible, was the emperor of ...
a) Russia
b) Sweden
c) Japan
d) Thailand

16. Who, along with Friedrich Engels, wrote *The Communist Manifesto*?
a) William Jones
b) Karl Marx
c) Jean-Jacques Rousseau
d) Montesquieu

17. Which famous incident occurred on 16 December 1773 at Griffin's Wharf, Massachusetts?
a) Boston Tea Party
b) Assassination of Martin Luther King, Jr

c) Sinking of the *Lusitania*
d) Battle of Gettysburg

18. Whose father, Nicomachus, was the physician of Alexander's grandfather?
a) Plato
b) Aristotle
c) Socrates
d) Galileo

19. In 1912, who was appointed editor of the newspaper *Avanti!*?
a) Adolf Hitler
b) Benito Mussolini
c) Winston Churchill
d) Joseph Pulitzer

20. Who was born as François-Marie Arouet?
a) Voltaire
b) Jean-Jacques Rousseau
c) Socrates
d) Confucius

ANSWERS

ART AND CULTURE

1. Lamp inside a pot
2. Odissi
3. Amjad Ali Khan
4. Koodiyattam
5. Tamil Nadu
6. Krishna
7. Horse
8. Mohiniattam
9. Rangoli
10. Ektara
11. West Bengal
12. White
13. Kathakali
14. Rice
15. Nataraja
16. One
    The *Mona Lisa.*
17. Qatar
18. Madhya Pradesh
19. Bhupen Hazarika
20. Bharatanatyam

ASTRONOMY

1. Earth
2. Saturn
3. West
4. Neptune
5. Galileo Galilei
6. Neptune

7. Jupiter
8. Venus
9. Neptune
10. Helium
11. Jupiter
12. Jantar Mantar
13. Neptune
14. Galileo Galilei
15. Nicolaus Copernicus
16. Taurus
17. The Great Bear
18. Asteroids
19. Uranus
20. Galileo Galilei

AWARDS

1. Classical music
2. M.F. Husain
3. Nelson Mandela
4. *My Name Is Khan*
5. Jnanpith Award
6. Sachin Tendulkar
7. Vinoba Bhave
8. Weavers
9. V.P. Singh
10. R.K. Narayan
11. Viswanathan Anand
12. Bismillah Khan
13. A.R. Rahman
14. C.N.R. Rao

15. Nargis Dutt
16. Param Vir Chakra
17. Rabindranath Tagore
18. Amitabh Bachchan
19. Ramon Magsaysay Award
20. Kalinga Prize

BOOKS AND AUTHORS

1. Rabindranath Tagore
2. Jawaharlal Nehru
   The Discovery of India
3. R.K. Laxman
4. Atharva Veda
5. Vikramaditya
6. Buddhism
7. Malgudi
8. *3 Idiots*
9. Kabir
10. Satyajit Ray
11. Perry Mason
12. *Alice's Adventures in Wonderland*
13. Man
14. *David Copperfield*
15. Robinson Crusoe Island
16. *Gulliver's Travels*
17. Sinbad
18. Woodcutter
19. *Treasure Island*
20. *The Lord of the Rings*

CLOTHES AND ACCESSORIES

1. Brass
2. Aquamarine
3. Silkworms
4. Diamond
5. Shoes
6. Moustaches
7. Manish Malhotra
8. Goat
9. Kilt
10. Head
    This traditional headgear is made of strips of bamboo.
11. Sherwani
12. Ankle
13. Pleated salwars
14. Surma
15. Head
16. Batik
17. Embroidery
18. Collars
19. Wool
    It comes from the Persian word *pašm*.
20. Cargos

CARTOONS AND COMICS

1. Hobbes
2. Batman
3. Pokémon
4. Spider-Man
5. Jupiter

6. Cyborg
7. Hulk
8. Iron Man
9. Chacha Chaudhary
10. Wolf
11. Jaggu
12. Batman
13. Fox terrier
14. Dog
15. Phantom
16. Botanix
17. Spider-Man
18. Mickey Mouse
19. Green Lantern
20. Garfield

COMPUTERS

1. EUROPE
2. Cursor
3. BASIC
4. Ctrl + S
5. Cortana
6. W
7. Encryption
8. Z
9. 7
10. Space bar
11. F1
12. Bug
13. Crash
14. Mickeys

15. Keyboards
16. Yahoo
17. CPU
18. Python
19. FORTRAN
20. Printer

CRICKET I

1. Duckworth-Lewis system
2. Virat Kohli
3. Dead ball
4. Ranjitsinhji
5. Virat Kohli
6. Lala Amarnath
7. Jhulan Goswami
8. Sachin Tendulkar
9. Nightwatchman
10. Mumbai Indians
11. Brian Lara
12. England
13. M.S. Dhoni
14. Willow
15. When a batsman is out on the first ball he faces
16. Mithali Raj
17. Gautam Gambhir
18. Bengaluru
19. M.S. Dhoni
    Mohammad Azharuddin—174 matches; Sourav Ganguly—146 matches; M.S. Dhoni—200 matches; Sachin Tendulkar—73 matches.
20. Donald Bradman

CRICKET II

1. Rajasthan Royals
2. Silly point
3. Brendon McCullum
4. Sourav Ganguly
5. Ricky Ponting
6. Two
7. Kane Williamson
8. Hyderabad
9. Rohit Sharma
10. Jasprit Bumrah
11. Rahul Dravid
12. *Patiala House*
13. Sachin Tendulkar
14. Chris Gayle
15. AB de Villiers
16. The pink ball
17. India and England
18. Kapil Dev
19. South Africa
20. Leg bye

DISEASES AND DISORDERS

1. Edward Jenner
2. The common cold
   Most adults have at least two to three colds each year, while children have as many as six to eight.
3. Liver diseases
4. Diabetes
5. Eyes

6. Tooth decay
7. Dentist
8. Tennis elbow
9. Rabies
10. Liver
11. Skin
12. Nervous system
13. Skin
14. Heart
15. Mumps
16. Blood sugar
17. Chikungunya
18. Cataract
19. Heart
20. Stomach

ECONOMY

1. Indian saris
2. The Chinese
3. Venezuela
4. Hyderabad
5. Tipu Sultan
6. Edmund Hillary
7. Mohur
8. India
9. Charminar
10. Muga silk
11. Coins
12. Pranab Mukherjee
13. China

14. Mauritius
15. Indira Gandhi
16. Banana
17. Ranjit Singh
18. Budget session
19. The postage stamp
20. Mulberry

ENTERTAINMENT

1. Amitabh Bachchan
2. *3 Idiots*
3. *Parineeta*
4. *Singh Is Kinng*
5. Aishwarya Rai
6. Hyderabad
7. Shammi Kapoor
8. Sonu Nigam
9. Peshwa Bajirao
10. Akshay Kumar
11. Salman Khan
12. Sridevi
13. Sonakshi Sinha
14. Kamal Haasan
15. Rajinikanth
16. A.R. Rahman
17. *Baahubali: The Beginning*
18. Star Wars
19. *The Great Gatsby*
20. Happy New Year

ENVIRONMENT

1. Greenpeace
2. Geneva
3. Bhutan
4. Compressed
5. Embrace
6. Tsunami
7. Mother Earth Day
8. 5 June
9. Wetlands
10. Rachel Carson
11. *WALL-E*
12. Fluorescent
13. Bhutan
14. Economy
15. Dachigam
16. The Amazon rainforest
17. Julia Roberts
18. Shah Rukh Khan
19. Haze
20. Desertification

FAMOUS WOMEN

1. M.S. Subbulakshmi
2. Amrita Pritam
3. Karnam Malleswari
4. Kiran Bedi
5. Mother Teresa
6. Indira Gandhi
7. Aishwarya Rai

8. She swam across the English Channel
9. Nur Jahan
10. Rani Lakshmibai
11. Razia Sultan
12. Shakuntala Devi
13. J. Jayalalithaa
14. Pratibha Patil
15. Mother
16. Vijaya Lakshmi Pandit
17. P.T. Usha
18. Governors of Indian states
19. Swami Vivekananda
20. Joan of Arc

FESTIVALS, FAIRS AND IMPORTANT DAYS

1. Diwali
2. Hornbill Festival
3. Diwali
4. Mizoram
5. Slides down chimneys
6. Saraswati
7. Rajasthan
8. Mahatma Gandhi
9. Krishna
10. Gujarat
11. September
12. Krishna
13. Swami Vivekananda
14. Diwali
15. Guru Nanak Dev

16. Onam
17. Pushkar Camel Fair
18. Saraswati
19. Atal Bihari Vajpayee
20. Buddha

FOOD I

1. Aniseed
2. Spanish
3. Orange
4. Cabbage
5. Jalebi
6. Potato
7. Ginger
8. Rajasthan
9. Gulab jamun
10. Besan
11. Tea
12. Mango
13. Pasta
14. Tibet
15. Basmati rice
16. Chow mein
17. Bihar
18. Saffron
19. Bangladesh
20. Wazwan

FOOD II

1. Thukpa

2. Coffee
3. Barfi
4. Ice cream
5. Shawarma
6. Grapes
7. Goa
8. Green
9. Pomegranate
10. Boiling
11. Chocolate
    The Aztecs called chocolate *xocoatl*.
12. Coffee
13. Orange
14. Pasta
15. Meat
16. Potato
17. Turmeric
18. Vada pav
19. Laddoo
20. Verghese Kurien

GEOGRAPHY OF INDIA

1. West Bengal
2. Sutlej
3. Andaman and Nicobar Islands
4. Arunachal Pradesh
5. Mountain passes
6. Visakhapatnam
7. Mahanadi
8. Uttar Pradesh

9. Eyes
10. Indus
11. Bihar
12. Kanchenjunga
13. Gujarat
14. Puducherry
15. Sutlej
16. Goa
17. Haridwar
18. The Siachen Glacier
19. Nagaland
20. Mount Everest

GREAT RULERS

1. Bairam Khan
2. Shah Jahan
3. Ashoka
4. Shivaji
5. Mauryan Empire
6. Babur
7. Shivaji
8. Alexander the Great
9. Peshwa
10. Buddhism
11. Qutbuddin Aibak
12. Mahavira
13. Alauddin Khilji
14. Kanishka
15. Maharana Pratap Singh of Mewar
16. Iltutmish

17. Akbar
18. Babur
19. Hyderabad
20. The Kohinoor

HINDI FILMS

1. Amitabh Bachchan
2. Rajkumar Hirani
3. Dhirubhai Ambani
4. Satyajit Ray
5. Abhishek Bachchan
6. Sonam Kapoor
7. Farhan Akhtar
8. Rajkummar Rao
9. Rangda
10. *Dangal*
11. Aditya Chopra
12. *Taare Zameen Par*
13. Zoya Akhtar
14. *Bunty Aur Babli*
15. Farah Khan
16. Ranbir Kapoor
17. Rahul Bose
18. *Maine Pyaar Kyun Kiya*
19. Deepika Padukone
20. *Dil Chahta Hai*

HINDU MYTHOLOGY

1. The first three Vedas
2. Vishwakarma

3. Gandhari
4. Lap
5. Ravana
6. Hanuman
7. Duryodhana
8. New Delhi
9. Sita
10. Eyes of the gods
11. Shakuntala
12. Ayodhya
13. Vishnu
14. Saraswati
15. Chitragupta
16. Musical instruments
17. Brahma
18. Arjuna
19. Rama
20. Shiva

HUMAN BODY

1. Eyes
2. Old people
3. Hands and feet
4. Small intestine
5. Ears
6. Iris
7. Hammer
8. Legs
9. Twenty-four
10. Tongue

11. Eyelids
12. Small intestine
13. Kidneys
14. Adam's apple
15. Blood
16. Pupils
17. Joints
18. Legs
19. Vitamin K
20. Radius

INDIA

1. Bhojpuri
   Currency notes have fifteen languages on the panel that appear on the reverse of the note.
2. Goa
3. Parliament House
4. Uttarakhand
5. Bengali
6. Shortest names of railway stations
7. 'Vande Mataram'
8. Namaskar
9. Speaker, Lok Sabha
10. K.M. Cariappa
11. Asiatic lion
12. Twelve
13. National flag
14. 22 March
15. CBI (Central Bureau of Investigation)
16. Ships

17. Rajasthan
18. Nashik
19. Sikkim
20. Brahmaputra

INDIAN HISTORY I

1. Dandi March
2. Dandi
3. The Grand Trunk Road
4. Cap
   He was popularly known as Tantia Tope.
5. Bhoodan
6. Chetak
7. Swaraj and Shaheed Islands
8. Kohima
9. Rani Lakshmibai
10. Mahatma Gandhi
11. Darjeeling
12. Shimla
13. Golden Temple
14. Pipal
15. Purana Qila
   Bara Darwaza, Humayun Gate and Talaqi Gate are the three gateways.
16. New Delhi
17. Maurya
18. Swami Vivekananda
19. Third Battle of Panipat
20. Buddha

INDIAN HISTORY II

1. The Arabian Sea
2. Prayagraj
3. Swami Vivekananda
4. Sarojini Naidu
5. Kautilya
6. Madurai
7. Shivaji
8. Buddhism
9. Yashodhara
10. Qutub Minar
11. Pallavas
12. Bihar
13. Rashtrakuta
14. Shah Jahan
15. Kerala
16. Panipat
17. Buland Darwaza
18. Richard Wellesley
19. Portuguese
20. Chand Bardai

LANGUAGE

1. English
2. Tarzan
3. Corridor
4. Tears of joy
5. Wing-foot
6. Nepali

7. Dictionary
8. Colon
9. Anagram
10. Plus
11. Spanish
12. William Shakespeare
'Foregone conclusion' in *Othello* and 'wild goose chase' in *Romeo and Juliet*.
13. Darjeeling
14. Hypodermic
15. Atlas
16. Arithmetic
17. Hindi
18. Kerala
Thiruvananthapuram.
19. Colon
20. Nelson

LEADERS

1. Jawaharlal Nehru
2. Theresa May
3. Winston Churchill
4. George Washington
5. Atal Bihari Vajpayee
6. Mahatma Gandhi
7. United States
8. Abul Kalam Azad
9. Mother Teresa
10. Winston Churchill
11. Russia

12. Theodore Roosevelt
13. Barack Obama
14. Bangladesh
15. Dalai Lama
16. Education
17. Satyagrahi
18. Adolf Hitler
19. Bhutan
20. Nelson Mandela

LITERATURE

1. Pig
2. Mumbai
3. *A Brief History of Time*
   Wings of Fire is the autobiography of A.P.J. Abdul Kalam, *Long Walk to Freedom* is the autobiographical work of Nelson Mandela and *The Diary of a Young Girl* is the autobiography of Anne Frank. Authored by Stephen Hawking, *A Brief History of Time* is known as a landmark volume in science writing.
4. Hamlet
5. *Treasure Island*
6. Gulliver
7. Suzanne Collins
8. William Shakespeare
9. *A Tale of Two Cities*
   It was written by Charles Dickens.
10. Amitav Ghosh
11. Panchatantra
12. Lord Voldemort
13. Hamlet

14. Alice
15. A prison
16. Panchatantra
17. Shylock
18. *Swami and Friends*
19. *Macbeth*
20. *The Jungle Book*

MIXED BAG I

1. Nelson Mandela
2. Passports
3. Potato
4. India
5. Sarson da saag
6. United States
7. Pakistan
8. Knots per square inch
9. Boat
10. Paper
11. Tea
12. Clutch
13. Louis Braille
14. Edmund Hillary
15. Teabags
16. Nepal
17. Green
18. Law
19. Popped popcorn
20. Brinjal

MIXED BAG II

1. Afghanistan
2. Red
3. Flamingo
4. Liver
5. United Nations
6. Prayagraj
7. Kidneys
8. Penguins
9. Teeth
10. Chhattisgarh
11. Rasmalai
12. Stomach
13. Brain
14. Arunachal Pradesh
15. Pancreas
16. Tomato
17. Nepal
18. Eyes
19. Chilli
20. China

MUSIC

1. Zakir Hussain
2. Amir Khusrau
3. Satyajit Ray
4. Zakir Hussain
5. Piano
6. Amjad Ali Khan
7. Sa

8. Ektara
9. Classical ragas
10. Duffli
11. Bansuri
12. Ravi Shankar
13. Violin
14. Shiv Kumar Sharma
15. Mridangam
16. Bhimsen Joshi
17. Ravi Shankar
18. Nagaswaram
19. The tabla
20. Mahatma Gandhi

MYTHOLOGY

1. Achilles
2. Athena
3. Thunderbolt
4. Poseidon
5. Greece
6. Venus
7. Mercury
8. Neptune
9. Lion
10. Pegasus
11. Theseus
12. Hydra
13. Medusa
14. Pandora
15. Valhalla
16. Friday

17. Seth
18. The sun god
19. Prometheus
20. Paris

NATURE

1. Cicada
2. Sundarbans
3. Northern Lights
4. Giant panda
5. Jim Corbett National Park
6. Coconut
7. Uluru
8. Cotton
9. Victoria Falls
10. Rubber
11. Indian rhinoceros
12. Maple
13. Glass bottle
14. Australia
15. Jim Corbett National Park
16. Bats
17. Grand Canyon
18. Coconut
19. Brazil
20. Mount Everest

NOBEL PRIZE

1. Rabindranath Tagore
2. Mother Teresa

3. S. Radhakrishnan
4. Four
   Woodrow Wilson, Theodore Roosevelt, Jimmy Carter and Barack Obama.
5. Literature
6. Mother Teresa
7. C.V. Raman
8. Three
9. Yemen
10. Chemistry
11. C.V. Raman
12. Insulin
13. Economic Sciences
14. Dynamite
15. Theodore Roosevelt
16. Peace
17. Robert Koch
18. S. Chandrasekhar
19. International Committee of the Red Cross
20. Malala Yousafzai

NUMBERS

1. Forty
2. 1 million
3. Twelve
4. Crore
5. Never
6. Seven
7. Four
8. Ten thousand

9. Forty days
10. Nothing
11. 40,000
12. Equals sign
13. Millennium
14. Duck
15. Twenty-one
16. Seven
17. November
18. Diamond jubilee
19. Thirteen
20. Thirteen

OLYMPIC GAMES

1. Tokyo
2. Sixteen
3. Olympic flag with five rings

   The five colours and white were chosen because they incorporated the colours of all national flags in existence at the time the Olympic flag was created.
4. Marathon

   26.2 miles.
5. Judo

   Developed from jujitsu, the hand-to-hand combat technique of ancient samurai warriors, judo basically involves throwing opponents to the floor and holding them in submission.
6. Shooting
7. Athletics
8. Badminton
9. Ice hockey

10. Metal ball
11. Polo
12. Swimming
13. Figure skating
14. Golf
15. Abhinav Bindra
16. World War I
17. Oldest medallist ever
18. Wrestling
19. Norway
20. Olympic motto

PLACES TO SEE

1. Statue of Liberty
2. India Gate
3. Rashtrapati Bhavan
4. Eiffel Tower
5. Gol Gumbaz
6. Jantar Mantar
7. Charminar
8. Eiffel Tower
9. Qutub Minar
10. Jantar Mantar
11. Statue of Liberty
12. Rashtrapati Bhavan
13. Ellora Caves
14. Humayun's Tomb
15. Bibi Ka Maqbara
16. Africa
17. Rajasthan

18. Five
19. Hawa Mahal
20. Taj Mahal

POLITICS

1. Manmohan Singh
2. S. Radhakrishnan
3. A.P.J. Abdul Kalam
4. Lal Bahadur Shastri
5. Rajiv Gandhi
6. Jawaharlal Nehru
7. Voting age
8. A charkha
The wheel, autographed in Hindi and English, was shipped some 12,000 miles and personally delivered to Ford by T.A. Raman in Greenfield Village, Michigan.
9. Prayagraj
10. Presidents of India
11. K.R. Narayanan
12. Viceroy
13. Thirty years
14. The vice president
15. K.R. Narayanan
16. Ministry of External Affairs
17. Riksdag
18. Gulzarilal Nanda
19. S. Radhakrishnan
20. Rajiv Gandhi

SCIENCE

1. Stethoscope
2. Equator
3. Blue
4. Holmium
5. Reflex
6. Microwave oven
7. Parasite
8. Total solar eclipse
9. P.C. Mahalanobis
10. Light
11. Alexander Graham Bell
12. Albert Einstein
13. A.P.J. Abdul Kalam
14. Gold
15. Albert Einstein
16. Francium
17. Candela
   Candela, unit of luminous intensity, from candle; Hertz, unit of frequency, from the name of H.R. Hertz; Pascal, unit of pressure, after Blaise Pascal; Watt, unit of power, after James Watt.
18. Ayurveda
19. Chlorine
20. Imagination

SPORTS I

1. Roger Federer
2. Three
3. ATK Mohun Bagan FC

4. Saina Nehwal
5. Boxing
6. Kabaddi
7. Cannot be ruled offside
8. Viswanathan Anand
9. Yellow
10. Kerala
11. US Open
12. Manchester United
13. P.T. Usha
14. Saina Nehwal
15. Yellow and red cards
16. Davis Cup
17. Narain Karthikeyan
18. Blue card
19. Li Na
20. Gymnastics

SPORTS II

1. Archery
2. Novak Djokovic
3. Raider
4. Usain Bolt
5. Queen
6. Billiards
7. Thomas Edison
8. Cycling
9. Coconut snatching
10. Zurich
11. Kabaddi
12. Lionel Messi

13. Table tennis
14. Blue
15. Featherweight
16. Cristiano Ronaldo
17. Kabaddi
18. Dwayne Bravo
19. M.C. Mary Kom
20. Score a goal

TECHNOLOGY

1. WhatsApp
2. A coffee pot
3. John Logie Baird
4. User interface
5. Ron Klein
6. China
7. Selfie
8. Temple Run
9. Megabyte
10. Hashtag
11. English
12. A camera
13. Kalpana Chawla
14. Afghanistan
15. Pac-Man
16. Retweet
17. PSY's 'Gangnam Style'
18. Larry
19. Tim Berners-Lee
20. Loudspeakers

TRAVEL

1. Malgudi Express
2. Panaji
3. Odisha
   It is in Bhubaneswar.
4. Sathya Sai Baba
5. Udaipur
6. Nepal
7. Charminar
8. Kanyakumari
9. Ahmedabad
10. Nagaland
11. B.R. Ambedkar
12. Maharashtra
13. AC Chair Car
14. Duronto
15. Sleeper
16. Amritsar
17. Maharashtra
18. Lucknow
19. None
20. Dehradun

WILDLIFE I

1. Penguin
   Gentoo penguins are the fastest underwater swimming birds
   and can reach speeds of 22 miles an hour.
2. Blue
3. Iceland

4. Ostrich
   Other than its long neck, it is known so because of its prominent eyes, sweeping eyelashes and its jolting walk.
5. Hummingbird
6. It is the smallest squirrel
7. Sangai
8. Irish wolfhound
   It is the tallest of all dog breeds.
9. Pashmina
10. Kangaroo
11. Cheetah
12. Kiwi
13. Cows
14. Ostrich
15. Kiwi
16. Komodo dragon
17. Head
18. Jellyfish
19. The insides of their mouth
20. Vampire bat

WILDLIFE II

1. Iguana
2. Dogs
3. Salamander
4. Eggs
5. Pelican
6. Giraffe
7. Greyhound
8. Spiders
9. Lion

10. Eyes
11. Ostrich
12. Aardvarks
13. Dinosaur
    It comes from the Greek words *deinos* (terrible) and *sauros* (lizard).
14. Cheetah
15. Great white shark
16. Ants
17. Giraffe
18. Jaguar
19. Kangaroos
20. Indian rhinoceros

THE WORLD AROUND US

1. Goa
2. Buddhism
3. Landing on the moon
4. Chef
5. Japan
6. Eiffel Tower
7. Andhra Pradesh
8. Maharashtra
9. Sleeping positions
10. President of India
11. Red
12. Mahatma and Kasturba Gandhi
13. West Bengal
14. Spain
15. Bhutan
16. India
17. Labour

18. Fingerprints
19. Mountaineering
20. Woodrow Wilson

WORLD GEOGRAPHY I

1. Taiga
2. Thar
3. The Netherlands
4. Winds
5. Andes
   It is the longest continental mountain range in the world.
6. Malaysia
7. Nepal
8. China
9. Tripura
10. Nile
11. The sunrise seen from Mount Fuji
12. Contour line
13. Africa
14. Mauritius
15. Antarctica
16. Pakistan
17. Nepal
18. Myanmar
19. China
20. Archipelago

WORLD GEOGRAPHY II

1. S
2. Asia

3. Bangladesh
4. Red Sea
5. Sri Lanka
6. Sahara
7. Antarctica
8. Jakarta
9. Bhutan
10. La Paz
11. Ural
12. Maldives
13. South America
14. Australia
15. Philippines
16. Sri Lanka
17. Australia
18. Mount Everest
19. Baghdad
20. Aurora borealis

WORLD HISTORY I

1. Nelson Mandela
2. Greece
3. October
4. Vasco da Gama
5. Adolf Hitler
6. Tipu Sultan
7. Leaning Tower of Pisa
8. King George VI
9. Florence Nightingale
10. Alexander the Great
11. France

12. Treaty of Versailles
13. Benito Mussolini
14. Christopher Columbus
15. August
16. Ho Chi Minh
17. Fa-hsien
18. Caligula
19. Nelson Mandela
20. Napoleonic Code

WORLD HISTORY II

1. Benjamin Franklin
2. Fa-hsien
3. Francis Drake
4. Thailand
5. France
6. Adolf Hitler
7. Khan Abdul Ghaffar Khan
8. Abraham Lincoln
9. China
10. Franklin Roosevelt
11. 116
12. Florence Nightingale
13. Tokyo
14. Richard Nixon
15. Russia
16. Karl Marx
17. Boston Tea Party
18. Aristotle
19. Benito Mussolini
20. Voltaire

The Best of Cadbury Bournvita Quiz Contest

For saving whose life was Nazm, a water bearer, crowned king for half a day at Agra Fort?

The literal meaning of which term in Latin is 'and the rest'?

Which Indian prime minister made a brief appearance in the 1977 film *Chala Murari Hero Ban Ne*?

How is muriatic acid better known?

Here are 1000 of the very best questions ever asked at the popular *Cadbury Bournvita Quiz Contest*!

It started as a radio quiz programme in 1972 and went on to become one of the most sought-after school quizzes in the country. On overwhelming public demand, BQC makes a comeback on television in 2011 and, with it, quizmaster Derek O'Brien brings you a compilation of 1000 questions from the archives of India's longest-running television game show. And just so you can be even more of a quiz whizz, there are 100 fun facts for you to know and enjoy.

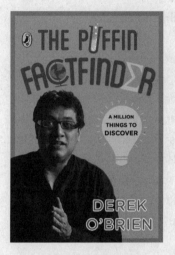

The Puffin Factfinder

Who was the first man to play golf on the moon?

Where would you weigh less—the equator or the North Pole?

What was the name of the poet known as the Parrot of India?

From Asia's best known quizmaster, Derek O'Brien, comes this ultimate reference book for students and inquisitive minds. Exhaustive and comprehensive, *The Puffin Factfinder* offers relevant information on everything you wanted to know. This handy book provides reliable and interesting information on a varied range of subjects, including history, geography, politics, science, literature, music, mathematics and more.

Here's your chance to get a low-down on anything—from historical anecdotes to global warming, the solar system to social networking. Comprising facts, figures, statistics and intriguing trivia, this indispensable reference book is ideal for schools, libraries and any quiz or trivia junkie.

READ MORE IN PUFFIN

The Bournvita Quiz Contest Collector's Edition: Volume 1

The edition for all quiz aficionados

The award-winning *Bournvita Quiz Contest* started as a radio programme in 1972, then shifted to television in the 1990s. Since 1994, it has been hosted by Asia's best-known quizmaster, Derek O'Brien, in his inimitable style. It holds the record for being the longest-running knowledge game show on Indian television.

This definitive edition comprises a selection of the best Q&As from the iconic children's show. Featuring 1000 questions, carefully curated from the exhaustive twenty-year-old archives, this book is dotted with heartening anecdotes, fun trivia and thoughtful essays by people who worked on this much-loved show.

The Wild Wisdom Quiz Book Volume 3

Discover the secrets of the wild with this all-new quiz book!

Delve deeper into the world of animals and plants with this indispensable quiz book that helps you explore our planet's natural beauty and myriad facets. Based on India's only international-level quiz on wildlife, *The Wild Wisdom Quiz Book Volume 3* is packed with exciting new Q & A on biomimicry, evolution, conservation heroes and more, and is interspersed with delightful illustrations. Learn about nature's creative cross-connections and hidden trump cards.

Relevant in today's changing world, this book tells you why it is high time we wise up, wipe the slate clean and achieve a perfect score with the New Deal for Nature and People by 2030 (more on this inside!). Budding wildlife lovers, nature explorers and avid quizzers, prepare yourself for a wild, wise ride!

'Young people are the future of our planet. We must equip them with the information, insight and practical skills to understand the importance of biodiversity, both intrinsically and for the survival of humanity'—David Attenborough